I0789475

ADULTS DON'T EXIST

Why No One Knows What They're Doing—and How to Think Anyway

Ken Konet, M.Ed., MBA

Humbolton Press

Copyright

© 2026 Ken Konet. All rights reserved.

Published by Humbolton Press.

No part of this publication may be reproduced, distributed, or transmitted in any form without prior written permission of the publisher, except for brief quotations in reviews.

ISBN (Paperback): 978-1-966703-22-8

Printed in the United States of America.

First Edition.

Table of Contents

For every kid who looked at a grown-up and thought,
"You have absolutely no idea what you're doing, do you?"

You were right.

*"The fundamental cause of the trouble
in the modern world today is that the
stupid are cocksure while the
intelligent are full of doubt."*
— Bertrand Russell

INTRODUCTION

The Software Update That Never Came

When I was seven years old, I watched my father try to fix the kitchen sink. He had a wrench in one hand, a YouTube tutorial playing on a phone balanced against the dish soap (except it was 1989, so replace "YouTube tutorial" with "a vague memory of something his father once said"), and the absolute confidence of a man who believed that turning forty had installed some kind of internal Home Repair Module in his brain.

Twenty minutes later, we had a geyser in the kitchen and my mother was on the phone with an actual plumber.

I learned something that day. Not about plumbing. About people.

Specifically, I learned that the adults in my life—the ones I trusted to navigate tax season, international conflicts, and the complex art of parallel parking—were, at their core, just bigger kids with credit cards and lower back pain.

* * *

We like to believe adulthood is a software update. Version 1.0: Child. Curious, confused, afraid of the dark. Version 2.0: Adult. Stable. Wise. Fully patched.

Unfortunately, adulthood is just Version 1.0 running on older hardware with better marketing.

Nobody tells you this. Not your parents, not your teachers, certainly not LinkedIn thought leaders who post things like "Leadership is a journey" next to a photo of themselves staring pensively at a lake. The entire infrastructure of civilization is built on a collective agreement that somewhere, somehow, somebody knows what they're doing.

Spoiler alert: they don't.

And that's actually wonderful news.

. . .

This isn't a cynical book. I need you to understand that upfront, because the title might suggest otherwise. I'm not here to tear anyone down or convince you that the world is a dumpster fire piloted by incompetent monkeys (though some days the evidence is compelling). I'm here to free you from the most destructive lie you've ever been told:

"Somebody else has it figured out."

Nobody has it figured out. Not your boss. Not the president. Not the surgeon who just saved your life (though we're really glad she studied). Not the billionaire on the magazine cover. Not the philosopher, the priest, or the guy on Reddit who is very, very certain about cryptocurrency.

Everyone—every single human who has ever drawn breath on this spinning rock—is improvising. Some of us just have nicer chairs.

. . .

What This Book Is (and Isn't)

This is a book about the beautiful, terrifying, hilarious reality that there is no finish line called "adulthood." There's no moment where the cosmic installer pops up and says, "Wisdom Package successfully downloaded. You are now qualified to make decisions."

Instead, what we get is experience. Some of it useful. Some of it just scar tissue shaped like lessons.

In these pages, we're going to look at some of the most celebrated, revered, supposedly "together" people in human history and discover that they were just as confused, scared, stubborn, and occasionally spectacularly wrong as the rest of us. We're going to dig into the psychology of why we build pedestals for people and then act shocked when they turn out to have human-sized feet. We're going to laugh. We're going to cringe. And hopefully, by the end, we're going to feel a lot less pressure to have it all figured out.

. . .

The Road Ahead

Here's how this book works. It's built in four parts, and each one does a different job.

Part I—The Lie We're Sold—dismantles the myth of the grown-up. We'll look at how society manufactures the illusion of adult authority, why your brain is wired to seek heroes, and how expertise in one domain gets mistaken for wisdom in all domains. By the end of Part I, you'll understand the machinery that creates the lie.

Part II—The Pedestal Graveyard—is where we meet the adults who weren't. Einstein, Newton, Edison, Steve Jobs, Oprah, Blockbuster, Theranos, and more. Geniuses who couldn't manage their own lives. Executives who missed the future while staring at it. Leaders who led us off cliffs while giving inspirational speeches about the view. These stories aren't here to make you feel superior. They're here to make you feel free.

Part III—Why We're All Like This—goes under the hood. Cognitive biases, ego protection, institutional failure, algorithmic manipulation, and the techniques that people use to exploit all of the above. This is the part that explains why the adults in Part II failed the way they did, and why you're vulnerable to the same failures.

Part IV—Building Something Better—gives you the tools. Not a guru to follow. Not a pedestal to build. A set of practical thinking frameworks—culminating in something I call the No-Adults Operating System—that work regardless of who's using them: how to evaluate ideas, detect false authority, think in probabilities, and make decisions that are better than your brain's default settings.

Because here's the real secret: the goal was never to become an "adult." The goal was to become a more honest version of the confused kid you've always been.

Let's get started. And maybe call a plumber.

PART I

THE LIE WE'RE SOLD

*"The only true wisdom is in knowing
you know nothing." — Socrates*

Chapter 1: The Myth of the Grown-Up

When Did You Expect It to Click?

Be honest. At some point in your life—maybe as a teenager staring at a pile of college applications, maybe at twenty-five when you realized you'd been eating cereal for dinner three nights a week, maybe at forty when your knee popped for no reason—you thought to yourself: "When does the adult thing kick in?"

You were waiting for the moment. The switch. The cosmic notification that reads: "Congratulations! You are now an adult. You will henceforth know how to respond to a wedding invitation, calculate a tip without your phone, and keep a plant alive for more than eleven days."

That notification never came. It never comes.

And it never will, because there is no such thing as an "adult" in the way we've been taught to understand the word.

· · ·

The concept of the "fully formed adult" is a social construction, not a biological event. Your body doesn't suddenly install wisdom at a particular age. What it installs is knee problems, a slower metabolism, and a deep emotional attachment to going to bed before ten.

Biologically, your prefrontal cortex—the part of the brain responsible for judgment, impulse control, and not texting your ex at 2 a.m.—doesn't fully develop until around age twenty-five. Neuroscientists at the National Institute of Mental Health have tracked this development through longitudinal brain imaging studies, and the findings are humbling: the last region to mature is the one responsible for weighing long-term consequences and regulating emotional impulses. Your brain literally prioritizes feeling over thinking for the first quarter-century of your existence. That's not a bug. That's the factory settings.

But even after twenty-five, "fully developed" doesn't mean "fully functional." It means the wiring is complete. What you do with that wiring is entirely up to you, your environment, your experiences, and approximately four hundred cognitive biases that we'll be exploring throughout this book. A fully wired brain is not a wise brain any more than a fully assembled car is a well-driven one. The hardware is there. The driver is still learning.

Society, on the other hand, tells a very different story. Society says: at eighteen, you can vote and go to war. At twenty-one, you can drink. At some vaguely defined point after that, you are expected to own furniture that didn't come in a flat-pack, understand your health insurance deductible, and have an opinion about mortgage rates.

None of this makes you an adult. It makes you a person who has been alive for a certain number of years and has accumulated enough administrative burdens to feel tired all the time.

• • •

The Authority Illusion

Here's where it gets interesting—and a little disturbing.

We don't just believe that adults exist. We need them to exist. Psychologically, we are wired to seek authority figures. It's a survival mechanism baked into our DNA from when our ancestors needed to follow the person who knew which berries would kill you and which ones were just okay.

Developmental psychologists have documented this extensively. Children naturally project omniscience onto their caregivers. "Mom and Dad know everything" isn't just a cute phase—it's a survival strategy that psychologists call the "omniscience assumption." Researcher Paul Harris at Harvard has shown that children as young as three selectively trust adults who have previously been accurate, but—and here's the critical finding—they default to trusting adults over their own perceptions when the two conflict. A child who can see with their own eyes that a cup is blue will agree that it's green if an adult says so with enough confidence.

We laugh at that. But we never fully outgrow it. We just transfer it. Instead of Mom and Dad, we project it onto bosses, politicians, celebrities, doctors, professors, coaches, pastors, and anyone with a corner office or a verified checkmark.

Stanley Milgram's obedience experiments in the 1960s showed just how deep this runs. In his most famous study, participants were instructed by a man in a lab coat to administer what they believed were increasingly dangerous electric shocks to a stranger in another room. The stranger—actually an actor—screamed, begged to stop, and eventually went silent. The man in the lab coat simply said, "The experiment requires you to continue."

Sixty-five percent of participants continued all the way to the maximum voltage. Not because they were sadists. Not because they lacked empathy—many of them were visibly distressed, sweating, trembling, and begging the experimenter to let them stop. They continued because a man in a lab coat told them to. The authority of the costume overrode their own moral judgment.

The lab coat. Not the science. Not the evidence. Not the qualifications. The outfit.

Milgram's experiments have been replicated across cultures and decades with remarkably consistent results. The obedience rate varies, but the core finding holds: humans defer to perceived authority even when that authority conflicts with their own values, their own observations, and their own conscience.

If that doesn't tell you everything about how we assign "adulthood" to people, nothing will.

. . .

The Pedestal Economy

We live in what I call the Pedestal Economy. It's an invisible marketplace where we trade our critical thinking for the comfort of believing someone else has the answers. The currency is trust, and we spend it like drunken sailors.

Think about it. How many times have you heard someone say, "Well, they're a doctor, so they must know what they're talking about"? Or, "They're the CEO, they must have a plan"? Or my personal favorite, "They wrote a book, so they're an expert"?

The Pedestal Economy works because it's efficient. Evaluating every claim on its own merit is exhausting. Psychologists call this cognitive load—the total amount of mental effort being used in your working memory. Your brain has limited processing capacity, and evaluating every claim from scratch would burn through it in minutes. So your brain developed shortcuts: instead of evaluating the message, evaluate the messenger. Do they seem credible? Do they have the right title? The right degree? Good enough. Move on.

These shortcuts work most of the time. The problem is that they work on a correlation that is increasingly unreliable: the assumption that credentials predict competence, that titles reflect ability, and that confidence indicates knowledge. In a world where those correlations held, the Pedestal Economy would be a perfectly rational system. In the world we actually live in—where confidence and competence are frequently divorced, where credentials can be earned without wisdom, and where the most visible people are often the most overconfident—the Pedestal Economy is a disaster engine.

The Pedestal Economy doesn't reward competence. It rewards confidence. And those are two very, very different things.

• • •

A Confession

I need to put my own skin in this game early, because this book doesn't work if I stand outside the problem pointing at other people.

I have three master's degrees. I've spent decades in corporate learning and development. I've designed training programs for Fortune 500 companies. And there was a period in my career—I'm not proud of it, but it's true—where I confused my credentials with competence in areas far beyond what those credentials actually covered.

I thought that because I understood how adults learn, I also understood how organizations should be run, how technology should be designed, and how roughly forty-seven other things worked. I didn't. I was a guy with expertise in one domain who had let the Pedestal Economy convince him that his pedestal was taller than it actually was.

My wife Izzy was the one who brought me back to earth. Not gently. Izzy doesn't do gently. She does accurate. And the most accurate thing she ever said to me was some version of: "You're really smart about learning design. You're not really smart about everything else. Sit down."

She was right. And that correction—delivered with the love and zero patience that only a spouse can provide—is essentially the thesis of this book, applied to everyone.

* * *

Your Move: Map Your Pedestal Economy

Here's your first exercise, and it's a simple one: identify your personal Pedestal Economy.

Think about the five people whose opinions you trust most. Not your closest friends—the people you defer to when you need to make a decision. Your financial advisor. Your doctor. Your boss. That podcast host. That author. That family member who always seems to have an answer.

Now ask yourself: why do I trust this person? Is it because I've independently evaluated their track record and found it reliable? Or is it because they have a title, a credential, a platform, or a confidence level that my brain interprets as authority?

You don't have to stop trusting them. Just notice why you trust them. That noticing—that tiny gap between automatic deference and conscious evaluation—is where this whole book lives. And it's where real thinking begins.

But before we can think clearly, we need to understand why we think so badly. Starting with the gap between how confident we feel and how competent we actually are—a gap so wide you could park a civilization in it.

Chapter 2: The Confidence-Competence Gap

Why the Loudest Person in the Room Is Usually the Least Qualified

In 1999, two psychologists at Cornell University—David Dunning and Justin Kruger—published a paper that would eventually become one of the most cited (and most misquoted) findings in modern psychology.

The study was elegantly simple. They gave participants tests in three areas: logical reasoning, grammar, and humor. Then they asked each participant to estimate how well they'd done compared to everyone else. The results were devastating. Participants who scored in the bottom quartile—the worst performers—estimated that they had scored, on average, in the sixty-second percentile. They thought they were solidly above average. Meanwhile, the best performers systematically underestimated their ability, assuming the tasks that were easy for them must be easy for everyone.

The finding was simple and devastating: people who are bad at something consistently overestimate how good they are at it, while people who are genuinely skilled tend to underestimate their ability. The less you know, the more certain you are that you know plenty. And the more you actually know, the more you realize how much you don't.

This is the Dunning-Kruger effect, and it is running the world.

The Science Beneath the Meme

The Dunning-Kruger effect has become a meme—a shorthand insult people deploy in online arguments to mean "you're too dumb to know you're dumb." But the actual science is both more nuanced and more interesting than the meme suggests.

Dunning and Kruger proposed that the effect is driven by a metacognitive deficit. Metacognition is thinking about thinking—the ability to monitor and evaluate your own cognitive processes. Their argument was that the skills needed to produce correct answers are the same skills needed to recognize correct answers. If you lack the skill, you lack the tool to detect that you lack the skill. It's a double curse: not only are you wrong, but you're missing the very equipment that would let you realize you're wrong.

The effect has been replicated across dozens of domains: medical diagnosis, driving ability, financial literacy, chess, debating, firearm safety, emotional intelligence. It appears cross-culturally, though the magnitude varies. It's been documented in professionals, not just students.

Now, in the interest of the intellectual honesty this book demands, I should note that the Dunning-Kruger effect has faced legitimate scientific criticism. Some researchers, including Gilles Gignac and Marcin Zajenkowski, have argued that much of the observed pattern can be explained by regression toward the mean—a statistical artifact rather than a psychological one. Their argument is that when you measure any two imperfectly correlated variables (actual performance and estimated performance), extreme scorers on one measure will tend to score closer to average on the other, which can create the appearance of overestimation and underestimation without any cognitive bias being involved.

Dunning and others have pushed back, arguing that while regression effects are real, they don't fully explain the data. The debate continues.

But here's what matters for this book: whether the Dunning-Kruger effect is a pure cognitive bias or a combination of cognitive and statistical factors, the observable phenomenon is real. People who know less tend to be more confident. People who know more tend to be more cautious. And our social systems—from corporate promotions to political elections to social media algorithms—systematically reward confidence over caution.

The mechanism is debatable. The outcome is not.

*　*　*

The Confidence-Competence Gap in the Wild

Let's make this painfully relatable. Think about the last time you were in a meeting and someone spoke with absolute, unshakable authority on a topic they clearly didn't understand. They used jargon. They spoke loudly. They made eye contact like a hostage negotiator. And everyone in the room nodded because confidence is a hell of a drug.

Meanwhile, the actual expert in the room stayed quiet, because they know enough to know it's complicated, and complicated doesn't play well in a conference room at 3 p.m. on a Tuesday.

I've been both people in this scenario. I've been the overconfident voice speaking beyond my expertise, and I've been the cautious one who knew the answer but couldn't compete with the volume. Early in my corporate career, I was more often the former. I had the energy of a man with two fresh MBAs and the certainty of someone who hadn't yet been wrong enough times to develop humility.

Experience fixed that. Or more accurately, failure fixed it. After enough confident predictions that turned out to be spectacularly wrong, I started developing what I now recognize as calibration—the ability to match my confidence level to my actual knowledge level. Calibration isn't something you're born with. It's scar tissue from being wrong in public.

The Overconfidence Effect

The Dunning-Kruger effect has a cousin, and his name is the Overconfidence Effect. This is the documented tendency for people to be more certain of their answers than their accuracy warrants. When people say they're "99 percent sure" about something, studies show they're wrong about 40 percent of the time.

Forty percent. That means nearly half of humanity's most confident declarations are objectively incorrect.

This isn't just about barroom arguments over sports statistics. This affects medicine, law, business, government, parenting, and literally every domain where decisions are made by humans. Pilots who overestimate their skills take unnecessary risks. Doctors who are too confident in a diagnosis miss the real problem. CEOs who confuse gut instinct with strategy drive companies off cliffs while posting motivational quotes about "trusting the process."

The overconfidence effect doesn't just explain individual errors. It explains entire systems of failure. It explains Enron. It explains the housing crash of 2008. It explains why Blockbuster looked at Netflix and said, "Nah, we're good."

. . .

The Imposter Syndrome Paradox

Here's the kicker, the beautiful, maddening irony of it all: if you've ever felt like a fraud—like you're faking it, like someday everyone will discover you have no idea what you're doing—

congratulations. That feeling is actually a sign that you're probably more competent than you think.

Imposter syndrome is the Dunning-Kruger effect in reverse. The more you know, the more you realize how much there is to know, and the more you worry you're not measuring up. Meanwhile, the person across the hall who has never cracked a book on the subject is sleeping like a baby because they're absolutely certain they've nailed it.

The world is being run by a strange combination of under-qualified people who feel incredibly qualified and over-qualified people who feel like frauds. This is not a comforting thought, but it's an honest one.

* * *

Your Move: Calibrate Your Confidence

Two exercises. Both uncomfortable.

First: the next time you feel very confident about something, treat that confidence as a data point, not a conclusion. Ask yourself: is my confidence based on evidence I've actually evaluated, or on a feeling of certainty that might just be the Dunning-Kruger effect doing its thing? The goal isn't to never feel confident. It's to check whether your confidence has earned its place.

Second: the next time you feel like a fraud, consider the possibility that the feeling itself is evidence of competence.

Not certainty—evidence. The people who worry about whether they're good enough are usually the ones who are. The ones who never worry are usually the ones who should.

And honesty—not confidence—is where real thinking begins.

But if the Confidence-Competence Gap explains why we're bad at evaluating ourselves, it doesn't fully explain why we're so eager to hand that evaluation over to someone else. For that, we need to go deeper—into the evolutionary wiring that makes us need heroes in the first place.

Chapter 3: Why We Need Heroes (and Why That's a Problem)

The Evolutionary Trap of Hero Worship

Somewhere deep in the machinery of your brain, there's a subroutine that's been running since the Paleolithic era. It goes something like this: "Find strong person. Follow strong person. Don't die."

That's it. That's the whole program. It was a terrific survival strategy fifty thousand years ago when "strong person" meant the one who knew where the water was or could fight off a saber-toothed cat. The problem is that this subroutine doesn't distinguish between "person who can save my life" and "person who gives confident TED Talks about disrupting the wellness space."

Hero worship is hardwired. And in the modern world, that wiring has become a liability.

The Safety Instinct

Psychologist Abraham Maslow put it elegantly in his hierarchy of needs: before we can worry about self-actualization and becoming our best selves, we need to feel safe. Safety, for most of human history, came from being near powerful people who seemed to know what they were doing. Chiefs, elders, priests, kings—the title changed, but the function was the same: someone to follow so we didn't have to figure everything out alone.

This isn't weakness. It's efficiency. Your brain can't independently evaluate every threat, every decision, every claim from scratch. Deferring to someone who's already figured it out—or who seems like they have—frees up cognitive resources for everything else. Evolutionary psychologists call this prestige bias: the tendency to copy, follow, and defer to individuals who appear successful or knowledgeable. Studies by Joseph Henrich and Francisco Gil-White have shown that prestige bias is a cross-cultural human universal—every society develops hierarchies of deference based on perceived competence.

The problem isn't that prestige bias exists. The problem is that "perceived competence" is an unreliable signal. It correlates with actual competence some of the time, but it also correlates with charisma, attractiveness, height, vocal depth, wealth, and the willingness to speak first and loudest. Your brain doesn't distinguish between these signals. It lumps them all into one category called "this person seems like they know what they're doing" and hands over the keys.

We've carried this instinct into the twenty-first century with almost zero modifications. We just substituted chiefs for CEOs, elders for influencers, and priests for anyone with a podcast and good lighting.

The result? An epidemic of misplaced trust. We hand over our critical thinking to people who look the part, sound the part, and market themselves well—not necessarily people who have earned the authority we've given them.

. . .

The Halo Effect: The Sneakiest Gremlin in Your Brain

There's a cognitive bias called the halo effect, and it's the cognitive engine that makes hero worship possible at scale.

Psychologist Edward Thorndike first documented it in 1920 while studying how military officers evaluated their soldiers. He found something strange: officers who rated a soldier as physically attractive also tended to rate that same soldier as more intelligent, more skilled, and more dependable. The positive impression in one area—appearance—was bleeding into every other evaluation, as if the soldier were surrounded by a halo of general goodness that colored everything about them.

Subsequent research has confirmed this effect across dozens of contexts. Attractive defendants receive lighter sentences. Taller candidates are more likely to win elections—a finding so consistent that political scientists have tracked it across decades of presidential races. People who are successful in one domain are assumed to be competent in domains they've never demonstrated knowledge of.

If someone is attractive, we unconsciously assume they're also smart, kind, and competent. If someone is successful in one field, we assume they must be wise in all fields. If someone can act, we assume they understand geopolitics. If someone can throw a ball really far, we assume they have valid opinions about breakfast cereal.

This is why movie stars sell watches. This is why athletes endorse insurance companies. This is why a tech billionaire's tweets about population decline carry more weight in public discourse than the actual demographers who study it. The halo doesn't care about domain specificity. It just radiates.

. . .

The Pedestal Construction Process

Here's how hero worship and the halo effect combine to construct pedestals in the modern world. A person achieves something genuinely impressive in one domain. Their achievement generates attention. The attention triggers the halo effect in observers. The halo effect makes the person seem competent in everything. Media outlets, seeking compelling voices, invite the person to comment on topics outside their expertise. The person, buoyed by their legitimate success and encouraged by the attention, complies. The audience, processing the confidence and credentials through the lens of the halo effect, accepts the commentary as authoritative.

The pedestal is now built. And it was built not out of the person's universal competence, but out of the audience's cognitive shortcuts.

This is the Pedestal Economy from Chapter 1, given a mechanism. The pedestals aren't built by the people standing on them. They're built by the rest of us, one unconscious assumption at a time.

. . .

Your Move: Spot the Halo

The halo effect operates below the threshold of conscious awareness, which means you can't just decide not to have it. But you can build a habit that partially compensates for it.

The habit is this: every time you find yourself impressed by a person—genuinely impressed, in a way that makes you want to listen to everything they say—pause and ask: what specifically impressed me? Was it their expertise in a relevant domain? Or was it something else—their appearance, their confidence, their success in an unrelated field, their platform size?

If the thing that impressed you isn't directly relevant to the thing they're currently talking about, you're experiencing the halo effect. The halo is real. The authority it implies is not.

Admire people for what they've actually earned. Just don't let that admiration leak into domains where they haven't earned anything. That's where the pedestals get dangerous—and as we're about to see in the next chapter, dangerous pedestals have a body count.

(In Part IV, we'll formalize this into what I call the No-Adults Operating System—a six-step process for evaluating any claim from any person. For now, just practice the noticing.)

Chapter 4: The Illusion of Expertise

"In the beginner's mind there are many possibilities, but in the expert's mind there are few." — Shunryu Suzuki

The Most Dangerous Person in Any Room

I need to tell you something that will sound counterintuitive, possibly offensive, and almost certainly true: the most dangerous person in any room is not the idiot. The idiot is easy to spot. The idiot announces themselves with bad takes and mismatched confidence, and everyone adjusts accordingly. You see the idiot coming, and you steer around them like a pothole on the highway.

No. The most dangerous person in the room is the expert who has wandered outside their lane and doesn't realize it.

Because this person isn't just confident—they've earned their confidence. They have the resume. The degrees. The track record. They've been right about so many things, for so long, that their brain has quietly upgraded "I'm good at this one thing" into "I'm good at understanding things in general." And once that upgrade installs? Watch out. Because now you've got a person whose expertise in one domain has metastasized into unearned authority in every domain, and nobody—including them—can tell the difference.

This is the Illusion of Expertise, and it has killed more people, crashed more companies, and derailed more good decisions than outright stupidity ever could.

. . .

Why Your Brain Can't Tell the Difference Between "Expert Here" and "Expert Everywhere"

Let me make this personal for a second. I'm a corporate instructional designer. I have three master's degrees. I've spent decades designing learning systems for Fortune 500 companies, figuring out how adults acquire skills, and building training programs that actually stick.

I'm good at that. Genuinely. I've earned that confidence through years of work, failure, revision, and the occasional moment where someone in a meeting says, "That actually worked," and I feel like I just found a twenty-dollar bill in an old jacket.

But here's what that expertise does not qualify me to do: diagnose your medical condition. Manage your investment portfolio. Rebuild your transmission. Advise you on immigration law. Fix my own plumbing (see: Introduction, kitchen geyser incident, still traumatized).

I know this. Intellectually, I know my expertise has boundaries. But my brain? My brain is not always so clear on the subject.

I once got a performance review—nineteen out of twenty categories rated "exceeds expectations." Glowing comments. A raise. A bonus. And one category—one—rated "meets expectations." Guess which part I obsessed over for three weeks? Not the nineteen things I crushed. The one category where I wasn't the expert. Because my brain had decided that being excellent in most areas meant I should be excellent in all areas. One "meets" felt like a personal attack, like someone had pointed at the edge of my competence and said, "Yeah, you're not actually that good over here."

It took my wife Izzy looking at me like I'd lost my entire mind and saying, "You got a raise and a bonus and you're upset because of one category?" for me to hear how absurd it sounded.

That's the Illusion of Expertise in miniature. My actual competence had created an expectation of universal competence, and the gap between the two felt like failure. Now imagine that same psychological process running in the brain of someone with considerably more power than a corporate instructional designer. A surgeon. A senator. A CEO. A Nobel laureate.

That's where things get dangerous.

Domain Specificity: The Science Your Brain Doesn't Want You to Know

Cognitive scientists have a term for this: domain specificity. It's the principle that expertise in one area does not automatically transfer to expertise in another. It sounds obvious when you say it out loud—of course a brilliant chemist isn't automatically qualified to design a bridge—but in practice, we violate this principle constantly.

Research on expert performance, particularly the work of K. Anders Ericsson (the guy behind the "10,000 hours" concept that Malcolm Gladwell popularized and slightly mangled), has consistently demonstrated that expertise is ruthlessly domain-specific. A chess grandmaster can look at a board mid-game and instantly see patterns that a novice would miss. But show that same grandmaster a random arrangement of pieces—positions that couldn't occur in an actual game—and their memory for the board drops to the same level as a beginner's. Their expertise isn't a general cognitive superpower. It's a highly specialized pattern-recognition system that only works within the specific domain where it was built.

41

This finding has been replicated across fields: medicine, music, sports, programming, firefighting. Experts develop mental models—complex internal representations of how their domain works—that allow them to process information faster and more accurately than novices. But those mental models are specific to the domain. A cardiologist's mental model of heart function is extraordinary. That same cardiologist's mental model of macroeconomics? No better than yours or mine. Possibly worse, because the confidence that comes from being brilliant in one domain can make you less cautious about shooting from the hip in another.

Philip Tetlock, the psychologist behind the landmark study on expert political predictions, found something devastating: experts asked to forecast events outside their specific area of expertise performed no better than random chance—and sometimes worse, because their confidence outpaced their accuracy. The experts who performed best were the ones who knew the boundaries of what they knew. The ones who performed worst were the ones who believed their expertise was a general-purpose tool.

Your brain, of course, does not come equipped with a helpful pop-up notification that says "Warning: you are now leaving your area of expertise. Confidence levels should be adjusted accordingly." If it did, half the op-eds ever written would never have been published, and Twitter would lose approximately ninety percent of its content.

The Night Before Challenger: When the Adults Overruled the Experts

If you want to understand the Illusion of Expertise at its most lethal, you need to understand what happened on the night of January 27, 1986—the night before the Space Shuttle Challenger exploded.

Here's what most people remember: the Challenger launched on an unusually cold Florida morning. Seventy-three seconds after liftoff, it broke apart. Seven astronauts died. Millions of Americans watched it happen live on television, including classrooms full of children who had tuned in to see schoolteacher Christa McAuliffe become the first civilian in space.

Here's what most people don't know: the disaster was preventable. And the reason it wasn't prevented is one of the most chilling case studies of the Illusion of Expertise ever documented.

The Challenger's solid rocket boosters were built by a company called Morton Thiokol, headquartered in Utah. The boosters were assembled in segments, and the joints between those segments were sealed by rubber O-rings—gaskets designed to prevent superheated gas from escaping during launch. Engineers at Thiokol had known for years that these O-rings had a potentially catastrophic design flaw. In cold temperatures, the rubber lost its flexibility, which compromised the seal. If the seal failed, hot gas would burn through the joint, and the booster would rupture.

Roger Boisjoly was one of those engineers. Six months before the Challenger launch, he wrote an internal memo to Thiokol's vice president of engineering that included a line so prescient it reads like prophecy: the result of an O-ring failure, he wrote, "would be a catastrophe of the highest order—loss of human life."

On the evening of January 27th, with temperatures at Cape Canaveral forecast to drop well below freezing overnight, Boisjoly and a group of Thiokol engineers convened an emergency teleconference with NASA managers. The engineers presented their data. They showed the correlation between cold temperatures and O-ring erosion. They recommended, clearly and unambiguously, that the launch be postponed until temperatures warmed.

NASA's response was not what you might expect from an organization whose entire mission depends on the safety of its astronauts.

Lawrence Mulloy, NASA's solid rocket booster project manager, reportedly pushed back hard. The launch had already been delayed multiple times. The media was watching. There was political pressure—the Reagan administration had heavily promoted the space program. One NASA manager reportedly said, "My God, Thiokol, when do you want me to launch—next April?"

What happened next is the part that should keep you up at night.

Morton Thiokol's management asked for a brief recess from the teleconference. During that recess, they held an internal meeting. And in that meeting, they did something unprecedented: they excluded their own engineers from the decision. The people who had designed the O-rings, who understood the data, who had been sounding the alarm for months—those people were removed from the room. The managers then reversed the engineering team's recommendation and told NASA that the data was "inconclusive" and the launch could proceed.

Allan McDonald, the director of Thiokol's booster rocket project, refused to sign the launch authorization. He was overruled. Boisjoly, watching his recommendation be discarded, later described the decision-making process as "an unethical forum resulting from intense customer intimidation."

The next morning, Challenger launched into a twenty-eight-degree Florida sky. The engineers at Thiokol's Utah headquarters watched the liftoff on television, holding their breath, half-expecting the shuttle to explode on the pad. When it cleared the launch tower, they felt a momentary wave of relief.

Seventy-three seconds later, that relief evaporated along with seven human lives.

• • •

The Expertise Inversion

Here's what makes the Challenger disaster a case study in the Illusion of Expertise rather than simple negligence: it wasn't that the decision-makers were stupid. They weren't. NASA managers were brilliant aerospace professionals. Thiokol's executives were accomplished leaders with decades of experience. These were adults. These were experts. These were exactly the kind of people we're supposed to trust when the stakes are this high.

But their expertise was in management, scheduling, politics, and program administration. Not in the materials science of O-ring behavior at sub-freezing temperatures. That expertise belonged to the engineers—the people who were physically removed from the room when the final decision was made.

This is what I call the Expertise Inversion: the phenomenon where the people with the most relevant knowledge are overruled by the people with the most organizational authority. It happens because our systems are designed to concentrate decision-making power in managers, executives, and leaders—people whose expertise is in running things, not in understanding things. And when those two kinds of

46

expertise conflict, organizational authority almost always wins.

Not because managers are malicious. But because authority confers confidence, and confidence looks exactly like competence to the human brain. The person with the title, the corner office, and the schedule pressure feels like the person who should be making the call. The engineer with the data and the fear in their eyes feels like the person who is being difficult.

Seven people died because the adults in the room were the wrong adults for the decision that needed to be made.

· · ·

The Doctor Who Killed Mothers by Refusing to Wash His Hands

The Challenger disaster is devastating. But at least it happened fast. What about when the Illusion of Expertise kills slowly, over years, while the experts responsible refuse to see what's right in front of them?

Let me introduce you to the most heartbreaking story you've probably never heard.

In the 1840s, a Hungarian physician named Ignaz Semmelweis was working at the Vienna General Hospital, which had two maternity clinics running side by side. One was staffed by doctors and medical students. The other was staffed

47

by midwives. The maternal death rate in the doctors' clinic was catastrophic—as high as one in six women admitted died of what was then called childbed fever. In the midwives' clinic? About one in fifty.

Women knew about this discrepancy. They begged to be admitted to the midwives' clinic. Some chose to give birth in the street rather than enter the doctors' ward, because the survival odds were literally better on a Viennese sidewalk than in the care of trained physicians.

Semmelweis investigated. He tested hypothesis after hypothesis—body position during birth, embarrassment from being examined by male doctors, even the possibility that the sound of a priest's bell passing through the ward was scaring women to death. Nothing held up. Until a colleague died after accidentally cutting himself during an autopsy and developing symptoms identical to childbed fever.

That's when Semmelweis put it together: the doctors were going directly from performing autopsies on corpses to examining pregnant women. Without washing their hands. They were literally carrying death from the dead to the living on their unwashed fingers.

He implemented a mandatory handwashing protocol using a chlorinated lime solution. Within months, the maternal death rate in the doctors' clinic dropped from roughly sixteen percent to under two percent. The data was immediate, dramatic, and undeniable.

And the medical establishment's response? They rejected it. Completely. Violently.

Not because the evidence was weak—it was overwhelming. Not because the solution was impractical—it was a bowl of chlorine water and thirty seconds of effort. They rejected it because accepting it would mean accepting something intolerable: that doctors—educated, credentialed, gentlemanly doctors—had been killing their own patients. That their expertise, their status, their identity as healers had been, in practice, an instrument of death.

Some doctors were literally offended by the suggestion that their hands could be unclean. Their social status as medical professionals was, in their minds, inconsistent with the possibility that they were carriers of disease. The idea that a junior physician from Hungary could see something they had missed was an assault not on their science but on their identity.

Semmelweis grew increasingly frustrated. He wrote open letters calling his colleagues "irresponsible murderers." He became erratic, confrontational, obsessive. In 1865, his colleagues committed him to an asylum. He died there fourteen days later, likely from injuries sustained at the hands of the guards.

Twenty years after Semmelweis's death, Louis Pasteur confirmed the germ theory of disease, and everything Semmelweis had demonstrated was vindicated. Handwashing became standard practice. The cognitive bias that caused his colleagues to reject his findings now bears his name: the Semmelweis Reflex—the automatic tendency to reject new evidence that contradicts established norms, beliefs, or professional identity.

The most knowledgeable people in the building killed women for decades because admitting they were wrong would have cost them something more precious than patients' lives: their self-image as experts.

. . .

The Expert-to-Pundit Pipeline

You don't have to go back to the nineteenth century or the Challenger disaster to see the Illusion of Expertise in action. It's happening right now, on your phone, in your podcast feed, and on the opinion pages of every major newspaper.

I call it the Expert-to-Pundit Pipeline, and it works like this: a person becomes genuinely accomplished in one field. They win awards. They publish papers. They build companies. Their expertise is real, earned, and legitimate. And then, because of the halo effect we discussed in the last chapter, the media starts asking them about everything else.

The Nobel Prize-winning physicist gets asked about economic policy. The tech billionaire gets asked about public health. The Oscar-winning actor gets asked about geopolitics. The retired general gets asked about climate science. And because these people are smart—because they're used to being right, used to being listened to, used to operating in a world that confirms their exceptional judgment—they answer. Confidently. Publicly. Often incorrectly.

Linus Pauling won two Nobel Prizes—one in Chemistry, one the Peace Prize. A towering intellect by any measure. He also spent the last decades of his life promoting massive doses of vitamin C as a cure for the common cold and a treatment for cancer, based on evidence that was, to put it charitably, thin. His medical recommendations were largely debunked, but because he was Linus Goddamn Pauling, people listened anyway. A two-time Nobel laureate's opinion on vitamin C carries more psychological weight than a thousand clinical trials, because our brains evaluate the messenger before the message.

This is domain specificity in reverse: instead of expertise being contained within its proper boundaries, it leaks—spilling over into areas where the expert has no more authority than your neighbor. But it doesn't look like leaking. It looks like wisdom. Because the person speaking has the credentials, the gravitas, and the institutional backing that our brains interpret as "this person knows things."

The Expert-to-Pundit Pipeline is how we end up living in a world where a podcast host with a background in martial arts commentary becomes one of America's most influential voices on epidemiology. Where a person who built a software company is treated as a leading authority on education reform. Where a reality television star can become a trusted source of medical advice because they have a large platform and unshakable confidence.

The pipeline doesn't require malice. It doesn't even require ego, though ego certainly helps. All it requires is a society that confuses authority in one domain with authority in general—which is exactly the society we've built.

. . .

The Thirty-Year Veteran Trap

There's a version of the Illusion of Expertise that doesn't involve Nobel laureates or space shuttles. It's quieter, more common, and it's probably happening in your workplace right now. I call it the Thirty-Year Veteran Trap, and it goes like this:

A person spends decades in a field. They accumulate experience, reputation, and seniority. They become the person everyone defers to. And at some point—slowly, almost imperceptibly—their experience stops being an asset and starts becoming a cage. Because the world changed, but their mental model didn't.

You've met this person. We all have. It's the doctor who prescribes the same treatment they learned in medical school thirty years ago, ignoring two decades of updated research because "I've been doing this longer than you've been alive." It's the manager who insists on processes that were cutting-edge in 2005 and are now actively counterproductive, but challenges feel like disrespect because seniority and expertise have merged in their mind into a single, unquestionable identity.

It's the technology executive who says "Nobody will ever want to watch movies on a phone" in 2007, because their thirty years of experience taught them that screens need to be big and living rooms need to be involved. Their experience was real. Their pattern recognition was real. But the patterns were from a world that no longer existed, and their confidence in those patterns was inversely proportional to their willingness to update them.

The Thirty-Year Veteran Trap is domain specificity hidden inside a timeline. The person's expertise was valid—once. In a specific context. Under specific conditions. But expertise has an expiration date, and most experts don't check the label. They assume that because they were right for thirty years, they're still right now. And the people around them, impressed by the track record, rarely push back hard enough to make them reconsider.

This is how entire industries get blindsided. Not by stupidity. By expertise that stayed still while the world kept moving.

The Corporate Training Irony (A Personal Confession)

I need to tell you something embarrassing, because this book doesn't work if I only point at other people's blind spots.

A few years ago, on what turned out to be one of the worst days of my life, I was literally standing on a stage teaching a corporate training session on resilience. I'd just delivered what I thought was a particularly brilliant segment on "how to bounce back from adversity"—complete with frameworks, case studies, and a nice tidy slide about "embracing the unexpected." I walked off the stage feeling like an authority on the subject. An expert on resilience. A man who had it figured out.

Then I checked my phone and found seventeen missed calls from my brother. My mom had a stroke.

And in that instant, every framework, every case study, every polished slide about resilience meant absolutely nothing. I wasn't an expert on adversity. I was a guy who'd read about adversity and organized it into bullet points. The actual experience of adversity—the panic, the helplessness, the impossible choice between being with my wife who needed me and flying to my mother who needed me—bore zero resemblance to anything in my training deck.

My expertise in teaching resilience did not make me an expert in experiencing resilience. Those are two entirely different domains. And it took the worst phone call of my life to teach me that.

The universe, as I mentioned, has a dark sense of humor.

I've Done This. You've Done This.

Let's not pretend this is a problem that only happens to other people.

I'm an instructional designer, which means I think about how people learn. I'm trained in it. I'm experienced in it. And because of that, I have a terrible habit of assuming that my understanding of how adults learn automatically makes me an authority on how organizations should be structured, how leaders should behave, how technology should be designed, and approximately forty-seven other topics where my actual expertise is, at best, adjacent.

I catch myself doing it. Sometimes. When Izzy gives me that look—the one that says, "You're doing the thing again where you think knowing one thing means you know all the things"— I usually recalibrate. But not always. Because the pull is strong. Once you've been right enough times in one area, your brain starts whispering, "You're probably right about this other thing, too."

And here's the insidious part: sometimes I am right about the other thing. Occasionally, peripheral knowledge does transfer. Occasionally, the pattern you see in your domain genuinely does apply to a different domain. And those occasional hits reinforce the belief that your expertise is broader than it actually is. It's confirmation bias weaponized by competence.

So the next time you hear a brilliant person say something confidently about a topic outside their field—whether that person is a Nobel laureate, a tech CEO, a surgeon, or a corporate instructional designer with three master's degrees and strong opinions about plumbing—remember this: their confidence is real. Their track record is real. And their expertise, in this particular moment, may be entirely irrelevant.

The Pattern

Here's your practical takeaway for this chapter, and it's a skill that will serve you every single day for the rest of your life:

Before you accept any claim from any person—no matter how impressive they are—ask yourself one question: "Is this person's expertise actually in this specific domain?"

Not "are they smart." Not "are they successful." Not "do they have credentials." But: is their expertise in the specific thing they're currently talking about?

A cardiologist telling you about your heart? Listen carefully. That same cardiologist telling you about cryptocurrency? They're just a person with an opinion and a stethoscope they aren't using.

A software engineer explaining their code architecture? Pay attention. That same engineer explaining geopolitical strategy? They're improvising with better vocabulary than most, but improvising all the same.

And when you catch yourself speaking with authority on a topic outside your lane—because you will, we all do—practice the most powerful sentence in the English language: "I don't actually know enough about this to have a strong opinion."

It feels like shrinking. It feels like admitting weakness. But it's actually the opposite. It's the moment you stop performing expertise and start practicing honesty. And honesty—real, uncomfortable, ego-bruising honesty—is the closest thing to actual adulthood that any of us will ever get.

Here are three things you can do this week to start building that muscle:

One: The next time someone impresses you with a confident opinion, pause and identify their actual domain of expertise. Then ask yourself: is what they're talking about inside that domain, or outside it? Don't change anything. Just notice. The noticing alone will start rewiring how you evaluate authority.

Two: Pick one opinion you hold strongly—about health, politics, money, parenting, anything—and ask yourself: where did I actually learn this? Did I learn it from someone with relevant expertise, or from someone who was just confident? Did I learn it from evidence, or from repetition? You don't have to change the opinion. But trace its origin. You might be surprised how many of your "strongest convictions" trace back to a charismatic person who happened to sound sure of themselves.

Three: The next time you feel the urge to weigh in on a topic outside your expertise—and you'll feel it, trust me, it's a strong pull—try saying this instead: "That's interesting. I don't know enough about it to have a real opinion, but I'd like to learn more." Watch what happens. People will respect you more, not less. Because in a world full of confident guessing, genuine intellectual humility is so rare that it registers as a superpower.

Roger Boisjoly knew the boundaries of his expertise. He knew O-rings. He knew temperature data. He knew what cold rubber does under pressure. And when the adults in the room—the managers, the executives, the schedule-keepers—overruled him, seven people died.

Ignaz Semmelweis knew the boundaries of his expertise. He knew mortality data. He knew that doctors who washed their hands stopped killing mothers. And when the adults in the room—the credentialed, the established, the offended—rejected him, thousands of women continued to die.

The illusion of expertise isn't just a cognitive curiosity. It's a body count.

And the only defense against it is the willingness to ask: "Do I actually know what I think I know? Or have I just been right often enough to stop checking?"

If you're asking that question, congratulations. You're closer to being a real adult than most of the experts on your television screen. And in Part IV, we'll turn that question into a repeatable system—the No-Adults Operating System—so you never have to rely on instinct alone again.

Not that real adults exist, of course. But you know what I mean.

PART II

THE PEDESTAL GRAVEYARD

*"Show me a hero and I'll write you a
tragedy."* — F. Scott Fitzgerald

Chapter 5: Geniuses Who Couldn't Get Out of Their Own Way

When Brilliant People Do Spectacularly Dumb Things

Let's start with the A-list. The people so smart that their names are synonymous with intelligence itself. Surely these folks had it figured out, right? They were the adults in the room, the ones who actually earned their pedestals?

Oh, sweet summer child. Buckle up.

· · ·

Albert Einstein: Genius at Physics, Disaster at Everything Else

Albert Einstein literally reimagined the fabric of space and time. His theory of general relativity is one of the pillars of modern physics. His name is a synonym for genius.

He was also, by nearly every account, a profoundly terrible husband and an absent father. In 1914, as his marriage to Mileva Marić was deteriorating, Einstein drafted a list of conditions she would need to accept to remain married to him. The document—preserved in his collected papers—included demands like "you will not expect any intimacy from me," "you will stop talking to me if I request it," and "you will leave my bedroom or study immediately without protest if I ask you to." It was less a marriage contract and more a hostage negotiation drafted by a physicist who'd never met a feeling he couldn't turn into an equation.

Mileva accepted the conditions. Then Einstein left her anyway, married his cousin Elsa, and spent the rest of his life as a serial philanderer whose romantic entanglements are documented in letters that make you wonder how a man who understood the curvature of spacetime couldn't understand the curvature of a human relationship.

His relationship with his sons was strained to the point of estrangement. His second son, Eduard, was diagnosed with schizophrenia and spent much of his adult life institutionalized. Einstein's response was largely to not respond—to keep a continent between them and hope the problem would resolve itself, like a thought experiment that someone else could finish.

Einstein also spent the last thirty years of his life chasing a unified field theory—a single equation to explain everything—and failed. Not because he wasn't smart enough, but because he refused to accept quantum mechanics, which he called "spooky action at a distance." The man who rewrote the laws of the universe couldn't accept that the universe didn't play by the rules he preferred. This is the Semmelweis Reflex wearing a Nobel Prize: when the evidence contradicts your worldview, it's the evidence that has to go.

Genius in one domain. Spectacularly human in everything else.

Isaac Newton: Inventor of Modern Physics, Investor in Financial Catastrophe

Isaac Newton invented calculus. He discovered the laws of motion and universal gravitation. He literally figured out why apples fall from trees and planets stay in orbit. If there's a Mount Rushmore of human intelligence, Newton's face is on it.

And yet, in 1720, Sir Isaac Newton—one of the most analytical minds in recorded history—invested heavily in the South Sea Company, a stock speculation bubble so obvious that even the coffee shops of London were buzzing with warnings. Newton initially invested early, made a handsome profit, and cashed out. Smart move. The smartest move.

Then he watched the stock keep climbing. And the sunk cost fallacy's cousin—the fear of missing out—grabbed him by the frontal cortex and said, "You clearly got out too early." So he reinvested. At the peak. With substantially more money than his original position. And rode it straight into the ground, losing roughly twenty thousand pounds—the equivalent of several million dollars today.

Afterward, Newton reportedly said, "I can calculate the motion of heavenly bodies, but not the madness of people." Which is a beautiful line, except that he wasn't observing the madness from outside. He was in it. He was the madness.

He also spent more time on alchemy and trying to decode the Book of Revelation than he ever did on physics. The father of modern science spent decades trying to turn lead into gold and predict the apocalypse. If that doesn't prove that genius and wisdom are completely different operating systems, nothing does.

• • •

Thomas Edison: The Man Who Electrocuted an Elephant to Win an Argument

Edison is the patron saint of perseverance. Ten thousand failed experiments before the light bulb, etc. What a trooper. What a legend.

He was also a ruthless businessman who went to bizarre and cruel lengths to discredit his rival, Nikola Tesla, and Tesla's alternating current (AC) electrical system. Edison's preferred direct current (DC) system was inferior—less efficient, couldn't travel long distances—but admitting that would have meant admitting he was wrong, and Thomas Edison would rather electrocute an elephant than do that.

I'm not being metaphorical. In 1903, Edison's associates publicly electrocuted an elephant named Topsy using AC current to "demonstrate" its dangers. The historical record is muddled on Edison's direct involvement, but the event was part of the broader "War of Currents" propaganda campaign his camp waged. Edison also championed the electric chair—

powered by AC, of course—as a way to associate his competitor's technology with death. He wanted people to call electrocution "being Westinghoused," after George Westinghouse, who backed Tesla's AC system.

Edison wasn't an idiot. He was a genius. But he was a genius who let ego override evidence—the same ego-protection mechanism we explored in the previous chapters. When your identity is built on being right, being wrong isn't just an error. It's an existential threat. And Edison would rather wage a propaganda war against the laws of physics than update his identity.

*   *   *

The Pattern

Notice the pattern across all three geniuses: domain-specific brilliance coupled with domain-general blindness. Einstein couldn't apply his analytical rigor to his own relationships. Newton couldn't apply his mathematical precision to financial markets. Edison couldn't apply his experimental method to his own ego.

These aren't failures of intelligence. They're failures of transfer. The cognitive biases we cataloged in Parts I and III don't skip geniuses. They hit geniuses harder, because geniuses have more ego invested in being right, more social reinforcement telling them they're exceptional, and more intellectual horsepower to construct elaborate rationalizations for their mistakes.

Intelligence is a tool. Like all tools, it works brilliantly for the job it was designed for and not at all for the jobs it wasn't. A scalpel is perfect for surgery. It's lousy for hammering nails. And a brain that can reimagine spacetime is not necessarily a brain that can manage a marriage, a portfolio, or its own ego.

Chapter 6: Titans of Business Who Fumbled the Future

When the Smartest People in the Room Missed What Was Right in Front of Them

If you want to understand how expertise expires, look no further than the boardroom. These are the people with the best data, the smartest advisors, the most expensive educations, and access to more information than any humans in history. And yet, the corporate landscape is littered with decisions so bad they could be taught as cautionary tales in kindergarten.

What connects every one of the following stories is the same cognitive pattern: success in the past creating overconfidence about the future. The Thirty-Year Veteran Trap, playing out at institutional scale.

. . .

Blockbuster vs. Netflix: The $6 Billion Shrug

In the year 2000, Reed Hastings and Marc Randolph walked into Blockbuster's Dallas headquarters and offered to sell Netflix for fifty million dollars. The Blockbuster CEO, John Antioco, reportedly nearly laughed them out of the room. Fifty million for a DVD-by-mail company? When Blockbuster had nine thousand stores and five billion dollars in annual revenue? Please.

Let me say that again for the people in the back. Fifty. Million. Dollars. For Netflix. In 2000.

As of this writing, Netflix is worth over two hundred billion dollars. Blockbuster is a single nostalgic store in Bend, Oregon, that mostly survives on ironic tourism and the lingering fumes of late fees past.

Here's what makes this a Pedestal Graveyard story and not just a bad business decision: Blockbuster's leadership wasn't stupid. They were experienced retail executives with decades of industry knowledge. They failed because the very expertise that made them successful—understanding how people rent physical media from physical stores—became the cage that prevented them from seeing a world where neither physical media nor physical stores would matter. Their expertise was real. It was just expiring.

. . .

Xerox PARC: Inventing the Future and Then Handing It Away

In the 1970s, researchers at Xerox's Palo Alto Research Center invented practically everything we associate with modern computing: the graphical user interface, the mouse, the desktop metaphor, WYSIWYG editing, Ethernet. They didn't just see the future—they built it.

And then Xerox's executives—the adults in the room—looked at these inventions and essentially said, "That's nice, but we sell copiers."

Steve Jobs visited Xerox PARC in 1979 and reportedly realized within minutes that he was looking at the future of computing. He later said that Xerox could have owned the entire computer industry. Instead, they kept selling toner.

This is the Expertise Inversion from Chapter 4, playing out in slow motion. The researchers who built the technology understood what it meant. The executives who controlled the budget understood copier margins. The people with the knowledge lacked the authority. The people with the authority lacked the vision. And the future walked out the door.

. . .

Yahoo: The Company That Said "No" to Everything

Yahoo once had the opportunity to buy Google for one million dollars. They passed. Later, Google came back and Yahoo offered three billion, but Google wanted five billion, and Yahoo balked. Then Microsoft offered to buy Yahoo for forty billion dollars, and Yahoo said no. Eventually, Yahoo sold its core business for roughly four and a half billion.

That's the business equivalent of finding a winning lottery ticket, throwing it away, finding another one, throwing it away, and then selling your house to cover the mortgage.

Every person in those boardrooms had an MBA, a corner office, and absolute confidence in their strategic vision. They were adults. They were leaders. They were supposed to know better. They didn't. Because no one ever does.

. . .

Decca Records: Rejecting the Beatles

On January 1, 1962, the Beatles auditioned for Decca Records. The band played fifteen songs. A&R executive Dick Rowe made his assessment: "Guitar groups are on the way out." He chose to sign the Tremeloes instead, partly because they were from London and wouldn't require travel expenses. The Beatles went on to become the best-selling music act of all time, earning an estimated thirty-eight and a half million dollars by the summer of 1967 alone.

Dick Rowe wasn't an amateur. He was a senior executive at one of the biggest record labels in the world. He had ears. He had experience. He had every resource to make the right call. And he still got it wrong in a way that would echo through decades. Not because he was incompetent. Because he was human.

. . .

Your Move: Check the Expiration Date

70

Every one of these business failures has the same structure: experts who were right about the past assumed they would be right about the future. Their track record became a prison. The next time someone tells you, "Trust me, I've been doing this for thirty years," remember: thirty years of experience is only valuable if the next thirty years look like the last thirty. And they almost never do.

Ask yourself: whose expertise in my life is based on a world that no longer exists? My financial advisor's? My industry mentor's? My own? The most dangerous expertise isn't the kind that's wrong. It's the kind that used to be right.

Chapter 7: Icons with Feet of Clay

When the People We Worship Turn Out to Be People

This chapter is going to be uncomfortable. Not because we're going to tear down heroes—we're going to humanize them. And humanizing people we've put on pedestals is always a little jarring, like finding out your favorite restaurant has a C health rating. The food's still good. But now you know about the kitchen.

The point of these stories isn't to diminish anyone's achievements. It's to demonstrate that achievement and wisdom are not the same thing—and that the halo effect tricks us into believing they are.

. . .

Steve Jobs: Visionary, Bully, and Fruitarian Cancer Patient

Steve Jobs co-founded Apple, revolutionized personal computing, and essentially invented the modern smartphone. He was, by any reasonable measure, one of the most influential people of the twentieth and twenty-first centuries.

He was also, by nearly every account from the people who worked with him, extraordinarily difficult. He parked in handicapped spaces. He screamed at employees until they cried. He denied paternity of his daughter Lisa for years—

while naming a computer after her—which is a level of emotional dysfunction that even a therapist would need a minute to process. Walter Isaacson's biography documents a man of extraordinary vision and extraordinary cruelty, often in the same meeting.

And then there's the cancer. In 2003, Jobs was diagnosed with a rare, slow-growing form of pancreatic cancer—a neuroendocrine tumor, which, with early surgery, had a substantially better prognosis than the more common and lethal pancreatic adenocarcinoma. Instead of pursuing immediate medical treatment, Jobs spent nine months exploring alternative therapies: juice fasts, acupuncture, herbal remedies, a fruitarian diet. By the time he agreed to surgery, the cancer had progressed.

This was a man who built a trillion-dollar company on rigorous design thinking and obsessive attention to detail. And when it came to the most important design challenge of all— his own survival—he tried to solve it with carrot juice. Not because he was stupid. Because the same personality traits that made him a visionary—the conviction that he could bend reality, the belief that rules didn't apply to him, the confidence that his instincts were superior to conventional wisdom—were catastrophically misapplied to a domain where conventional wisdom was backed by decades of oncological evidence.

The halo effect in its most lethal form: a man so successful in one domain that he believed his judgment was universal. And nobody around him—surrounded as he was by the social reinforcement loop of wealth, fame, and sycophancy—told him otherwise until it was too late.

. . .

Walt Disney: Fired for Lacking Imagination

Before he built the most recognizable entertainment empire on Earth, Walt Disney was fired from a newspaper job at the Kansas City Star. The editor's assessment? He "lacked imagination and had no good ideas."

Disney went on to go bankrupt with his first animation studio, Laugh-O-Gram. He couldn't pay rent. He reportedly survived on dog food at one point. The man who would become synonymous with magic and wonder was at one point eating kibble and sleeping in his office.

Disney's story isn't just about talent triumphing over adversity. It's about the unreliability of expert evaluation. The people who assessed Disney—the adults, the gatekeepers— looked at one of the most imaginative humans who would ever live and saw nothing. Their expertise in evaluating talent was real. Their application of it was catastrophically wrong. And they were wrong with total confidence.

. . .

Oprah Winfrey: Too Emotional for News (Thank God)

Oprah Winfrey was fired from her first television job as a news anchor in Baltimore. The reason? She was "too emotionally invested" in her stories. The executives who fired her looked at Oprah Winfrey—Oprah Winfrey—and decided she wasn't cut out for television.

The quality that got her fired—emotional investment—became the foundation of a media empire worth billions. She later reflected that the firing was one of the best things that ever happened to her, because it pushed her away from a format that suppressed her greatest strength and toward one that amplified it.

Turns out the thing that makes you "wrong" in one room might be the thing that makes you irreplaceable in another. But the adults in the room didn't see that.

● ● ●

Your Move: Question Your Framework

The next time you evaluate someone—a job candidate, a student, a colleague, your own kid—ask yourself: am I seeing this person clearly, or am I seeing them through a frame that might be wrong? The editors who rejected Disney. The executives who fired Oprah. The publishers who passed on Rowling. They weren't stupid. They were evaluating people through frameworks that didn't have room for what those people actually were.

Your frameworks might be doing the same thing right now. And you'd never know, because the people you've underestimated don't send you a notification when they prove you wrong. They just go prove you wrong somewhere else.

Chapter 8: Leaders Who Led Us Off a Cliff

The Myth of the Competent Authority

If there's one place where we desperately want adults to exist, it's in leadership. We want to believe that the people making decisions about our economies, our armies, our laws, and our institutions have some special qualification beyond "they wanted the job and were willing to campaign for it."

Spoiler: they usually don't. Leadership selects for ambition, charisma, and political skill. Not for judgment, wisdom, or the ability to say, "I don't know." The qualities that get you into the room are not the same qualities that make good decisions once you're there.

. . .

Neville Chamberlain: The Man Who Trusted the Most Untrustworthy Person in History

In 1938, British Prime Minister Neville Chamberlain flew to Munich, met with Adolf Hitler, and returned waving a signed agreement and declaring "peace for our time." He had, he believed, negotiated a lasting peace with Nazi Germany through the art of reasonable diplomacy.

One year later, World War II began.

Chamberlain wasn't a fool. He was an experienced politician, a former Chancellor of the Exchequer, and a man who genuinely believed that war could be prevented through negotiation. His mistake wasn't ignorance—it was an excess of a very particular kind of confidence: the belief that his judgment of character was sound. He looked at one of history's most transparent villains and thought, "I can work with this guy." He projected his own rationality onto someone who did not share it—a cognitive error psychologists call the false consensus effect.

This is what happens when we believe in adults. We assume that people in positions of power have some superior capacity for judgment. They don't. They have the same biases, the same wishful thinking, and the same tendency to see what they want to see. They just do it with bigger consequences.

. . .

The Fyre Festival: Dunning-Kruger Goes to the Bahamas

In 2017, entrepreneur Billy McFarland convinced investors, influencers, and thousands of ticket-buyers that he was about to throw the most exclusive, luxurious music festival in history on a private island in the Bahamas.

What they got were disaster relief tents, cheese sandwiches in styrofoam containers, feral dogs, and no music.

McFarland had zero event-planning experience. Zero. But he had something far more valuable than competence: he had confidence. He had a vision deck. He had Bella Hadid in a promotional video. He had a room full of adult investors who wrote checks because the presentation looked professional and questioning it would mean admitting they hadn't done their due diligence.

Fyre Festival is the Dunning-Kruger effect in its purest, most Instagram-filtered form—enabled by every concept in this book: the halo effect (celebrity endorsements), social proof (influencer marketing), the algorithm (viral promotion), and the Pedestal Economy (nobody questioning the confident guy with the nice deck). McFarland eventually went to prison. The investors got their money back. The people who bought tickets got a documentary and a cautionary tale.

• • •

Theranos: When a Turtleneck Becomes a Credential

Elizabeth Holmes dropped out of Stanford at nineteen and founded Theranos, a company that claimed to have revolutionized blood testing. The technology didn't work. It never worked. But Holmes had something better than working technology: she had the look, the narrative, and the turtleneck.

She convinced some of the most accomplished adults in America to join her board: Henry Kissinger, George Shultz, James Mattis, Sam Nunn. These were not naïve people. These were former Secretaries of State, Secretaries of Defense, and decorated senators. They were the very definition of "adults in the room."

And they were duped. Not because Holmes was the greatest con artist in history, but because the board members' expertise was in geopolitics and military strategy, not in medical technology. They were susceptible to the same Illusion of Expertise we explored in Chapter 4—their authority in one domain made them feel authoritative in all domains, and their prestige made it socially uncomfortable for anyone to question whether they actually understood the product.

Holmes was eventually convicted of fraud. But the deeper lesson isn't about one deceptive founder. It's about a system of credentialed adults who trusted confidence over evidence because that's what credentialed adults have always done.

• • •

Your Move: Build a Dissent Channel

The common thread in Chamberlain, McFarland, and Holmes isn't that they were uniquely evil or stupid. It's that the systems around them—political, financial, social—were designed to reward confidence and punish doubt. Nobody got promoted for saying, "I'm not sure about this." Nobody got funded for saying, "The evidence is mixed." Nobody got elected for saying, "I might be wrong."

If you're in a position of authority—any authority, from parenting to management to politics—ask yourself: have I built a system where people can safely tell me I'm wrong? If the answer is no, you're not leading. You're performing. And the performance will end the way it always ends: with consequences that the audience didn't sign up for.

Chapter 9: Creative Geniuses and Their Spectacular Messes

Art, Madness, and the Myth of the Tortured Genius

There's a romantic idea that creative genius comes paired with some kind of deeper understanding of the human condition. That artists, writers, and musicians see the world more clearly than the rest of us. That their brilliance illuminates some path to truth.

And sometimes it does. But other times, it illuminates a path straight into a dumpster. And the halo effect means we often can't tell which is which until we're already following.

. . .

F. Scott Fitzgerald: Literary Genius, Terrible Partner

F. Scott Fitzgerald wrote The Great Gatsby, one of the most celebrated novels in American literature. He captured the excess, the longing, and the hollow center of the American Dream with prose so precise it feels like surgery.

He was also, by most accounts, a raging alcoholic who was jealous of his wife Zelda's talent and allegedly stole from her diary to fuel his own work. Zelda herself noted the borrowing publicly, writing in a review of his novel The Beautiful and Damned that "Mr. Fitzgerald seems to believe that plagiarism begins at home." Their marriage was a mutual destruction pact wrapped in Jazz Age glamour.

Fitzgerald understood the human condition on paper. In practice, he was financially reckless, emotionally volatile, and so deep in the bottle that his later works had to be pieced together from fragments by editors. He died at forty-four believing he was a failure, at a time when The Great Gatsby was out of print and selling poorly.

The man who wrote the definitive book about the emptiness of pursuing the wrong dream spent his own life doing exactly that. If that's not proof that understanding something intellectually and actually applying it are two different skills, nothing is.

. . .

Stephen King: Thirty Rejections for the Most Successful Horror Career in History

Stephen King's first novel, Carrie, was rejected thirty times. Thirty different publishers read the manuscript, evaluated it with their professional expertise, and concluded: nah, this isn't it. One editor reportedly told him that "negative utopias" didn't sell.

King threw the manuscript in the trash. His wife, Tabitha, fished it out and told him to resubmit it. He did. The eventual publisher gave him a twenty-five-hundred-dollar advance—

modest even by 1973 standards. The paperback rights then sold for four hundred thousand dollars.

The rest is a career spanning over sixty novels, three hundred and fifty million books sold, and a body of work that has defined the horror genre for half a century.

Thirty professional editors—adults, experts, people whose entire job was identifying publishable talent—looked at one of the most commercially successful authors who would ever live and said, "Pass." Thank God for Tabitha King, the only actual adult in that story.

. . .

J.K. Rowling: Twelve Publishers Who Didn't Want to Print Money

Before Harry Potter became a multi-billion-dollar franchise, the manuscript was rejected by twelve publishers. Twelve groups of professional adults whose literal job was to identify books that would sell looked at the most commercially successful book series of the modern era and thought, "This isn't marketable." One editor reportedly advised Rowling to get a day job.

Rowling was a single mother on government assistance, writing in cafes while her baby slept. She had every reason to believe the experts were right and she was delusional. The adults had spoken. The system had evaluated her work and rendered its judgment.

The system was wrong. Because the system is made of people. And people don't magically become infallible because they have a title and an office.

. . .

Your Move: The Creator2019s Dilemma

If you're creating something—writing, building, designing, inventing—and the "experts" have told you it won't work, consider the possibility that they're right. Most rejected work is rejected for good reasons. But also consider the possibility that their framework doesn't have room for what you're offering. Disney was evaluated by people who couldn't see animation. King was evaluated by people who didn't believe in horror. Rowling was evaluated by people who thought children's fantasy was a dead market.

The question isn't whether the experts might be wrong. It's whether you've honestly evaluated whether they're wrong about you specifically, or whether you're just using their wrongness about someone else as an excuse to avoid confronting legitimate feedback. That distinction—between valid rejection of the status quo and ego-driven refusal to accept criticism—is one of the hardest in all of human thinking. And adults, as we've established, don't exist to make it for you.

PART III

WHY WE'RE ALL LIKE THIS

"We are all in the gutter, but some of us are looking at the stars." — Oscar Wilde

Chapter 10: Your Brain Is Lying to You (And It's Really Good at It)

A Field Guide to Your Own Cognitive Disasters

If the first nine chapters have established anything, it's that even the smartest, most accomplished, most experienced humans on the planet make spectacularly bad decisions. The question isn't whether these people were flawed—it's why. What's going on under the hood that makes Homo sapiens so reliably unreliable?

The answer is cognitive biases—systematic errors in thinking that affect every human brain, regardless of IQ, education, or how many TED Talks you've watched. These aren't bugs in the system. They're features. Your brain developed these shortcuts to help you survive, and for the most part, they worked brilliantly for hundreds of thousands of years. The problem is that the world has changed a lot faster than your brain has.

What follows is a field guide to the biases that are most relevant to this book's thesis. This isn't a complete list—psychologists have cataloged over two hundred cognitive biases, which is itself a depressing commentary on human cognition. But these are the ones that most directly explain why we build pedestals, why we trust confidence over competence, and why the adults we rely on keep turning out to be just as lost as the rest of us.

Confirmation Bias: The Google Search of the Mind

Confirmation bias is the tendency to seek out, remember, and favor information that supports what you already believe while ignoring or discounting information that contradicts it. It's like having a search engine in your head that only returns results you agree with.

This is why your uncle can watch the same news event as you and come away with the exact opposite conclusion. It's why flat-earthers exist. It's why people who have been wrong about a prediction for ten years will point to the one time something vaguely aligned with their forecast and say, "See? I told you so."

The research on confirmation bias is vast and deeply unsettling. In one classic study, researchers gave participants a set of evidence about the death penalty's effectiveness as a deterrent. The evidence was mixed—some supporting deterrence, some refuting it. After reading the same evidence, participants who initially supported the death penalty became more confident in their support, and participants who initially opposed it became more confident in their opposition. The same data pushed people in opposite directions, depending on where they started. The evidence didn't change minds. It strengthened whatever mind was already there.

And here's the part that should scare you: confirmation bias doesn't care how smart you are. In fact, some research suggests that smarter people are actually better at finding clever justifications for their existing beliefs, making them more susceptible, not less. Intelligence doesn't defeat bias. It just gives bias better ammunition.

* * *

Survivorship Bias: The Ghost Stories We Don't Tell

During World War II, the military analyzed the bullet holes in planes that returned from missions and considered adding armor to the most-hit areas. Statistician Abraham Wald pointed out the critical flaw: they were only looking at the planes that made it back. The planes that didn't return were the ones hit in the areas without holes—those were the critical spots that needed armor.

This is survivorship bias—the tendency to focus on the winners and draw conclusions from their stories while completely ignoring the far more numerous losers.

Every inspirational business book does this. "Steve Jobs dropped out of college and became a billionaire!" Yes. And millions of other people dropped out of college and did not become billionaires. We don't write books about them. We don't analyze their strategies. They're invisible. We study the bullet holes on the planes that came home and call it wisdom.

I'm acutely aware of this bias because I'm an author. The stories I've told in this book are all stories of visible people—people who succeeded, or who failed visibly enough to make the history books. But for every Einstein who rejected quantum mechanics and stayed famous anyway, there are thousands of scientists who rejected new evidence and faded into obscurity. For every Oprah who got fired and built an empire, there are millions who got fired and just... stayed fired. The survivors tell a story that feels like a lesson. But the lesson is incomplete, because we're missing the data from everyone who didn't survive.

Keep that in mind as you read the rest of this book. Including this chapter. Especially this chapter.

. . .

The Sunk Cost Fallacy: Why You Finished That Terrible Movie

The sunk cost fallacy is the tendency to continue investing in something because of what you've already invested, rather than because of what you're likely to gain. It's why you sat through the entire two-hour-and-forty-minute director's cut of a movie you hated after the first twenty minutes—because you already paid fourteen dollars for the ticket.

It's also why people stay in bad jobs, bad relationships, and bad investments long after the evidence is screaming at them to leave. "But I've already put in five years!" Yes. And you can't get those five years back. The only question that matters is whether the next year will be worth it, and your past investment has absolutely no bearing on that answer.

I'll confess to a sunk cost fallacy that cost me years. Early in my career, I spent an enormous amount of time building expertise in a technology platform that was clearly being phased out. I could see the writing on the wall. Colleagues were migrating to newer tools. The industry was moving. But I'd invested so much time mastering this platform that switching felt like throwing all that expertise away. So I stayed. And stayed. And stayed. Until the platform was basically dead and I had to learn the new thing anyway— except now I was behind everyone who'd made the switch two years earlier.

I didn't stay because I thought the old platform would survive. I stayed because leaving felt like admitting I'd wasted my time. And admitting you've wasted time feels worse than actually wasting more time. That's not adulthood. That's ego management wearing a business-casual costume.

• • •

Anchoring: The First Number Wins

Anchoring is the cognitive bias that causes us to rely too heavily on the first piece of information we receive. In negotiations, the first number on the table disproportionately influences the final outcome, regardless of whether that number is reasonable.

In a famous study by Tversky and Kahneman, participants watched a roulette wheel land on either ten or sixty-five (the wheel was rigged). Then they were asked to estimate what percentage of African countries are members of the United Nations. Participants who saw the wheel land on ten guessed, on average, twenty-five percent. Those who saw sixty-five guessed forty-five percent. A completely random, irrelevant number on a roulette wheel shifted their estimates of a factual question by twenty percentage points. The anchor doesn't even have to be related to the question. It just has to arrive first.

This is why car salespeople always start with a high price. This is why stores show the "original price" crossed out next to the sale price. This is why a house listed at six hundred thousand feels like a bargain after you've toured houses at eight hundred thousand, even if the house is objectively worth four hundred.

Every "adult" decision you've ever made—every salary negotiation, every major purchase, every budget you've set— has been influenced by anchoring. You didn't arrive at those numbers through rational analysis. You arrived at them because some number came first, and your brain latched onto it like a puppy with a sock.

● ● ●

Your Move: Four Biases, Four Pause Points

You can't eliminate cognitive biases. They're hardwired. But you can build awareness of the specific situations where they're most likely to fire, and develop the habit of pausing when you recognize those situations.

When you feel certain you're right: that's confirmation bias territory. Check for disconfirming evidence.

When you're drawing lessons from success stories: that's survivorship bias territory. Ask who's missing from the story.

When you're continuing something because you've already invested: that's sunk cost territory. Evaluate the future, not the past.

When you're evaluating a number or an offer: that's anchoring territory. Ask what your estimate would be if you hadn't seen the first number.

Four biases. Four pause points. Start there. It won't make you immune, but it'll make you dangerous—to the biases, not to yourself. These pause points become Steps 1 and 3 of the No-Adults Operating System you'll build in Chapter 19: Pause before reacting, then check the evidence before committing.

Chapter 11: The Ego Problem

Why Admitting You're Wrong Feels Like Dying

There is a reason the smartest people in every chapter of this book made the dumbest decisions, and it's not just cognitive biases. It's something far more primal, far more deeply embedded in the human experience.

It's ego.

Not ego in the pop-psychology, "that guy has a big ego" sense. Ego in the fundamental sense: your brain's desperate, constant, never-ending campaign to protect the story it tells about who you are.

Cognitive Dissonance: The War Inside Your Head

Psychologists call it cognitive dissonance—the mental discomfort you experience when you hold two contradictory beliefs at the same time. Leon Festinger first described it in 1957, and his research revealed something that should make every rational person deeply uncomfortable: when confronted with evidence that contradicts a deeply held belief, most people don't change the belief. They change their interpretation of the evidence.

Festinger studied a cult that had predicted the end of the world on a specific date. When the date passed and the world stubbornly continued to exist, the cult members didn't abandon their belief. They doubled down, claiming that their faith had saved the world. The disconfirming evidence—the world literally not ending—was reinterpreted as confirming evidence. That's how powerful cognitive dissonance is. It can turn proof that you're wrong into proof that you're right.

In everyday life, it looks like this: "I am a smart, capable person" plus "I just made a really stupid decision" equals unbearable mental tension. One of them has to go. And if you're like most humans (and you are), your brain will work overtime to resolve the conflict by changing the second belief. "I didn't make a stupid decision. I was working with bad information. The market was unpredictable. Nobody could have seen that coming. Also, Mercury was in retrograde."

Anything—anything—is preferable to accepting the simple truth: I was wrong.

. . .

The Identity Threat

This isn't vanity. It's survival. Your sense of identity—your understanding of who you are, what you're good at, and where you fit in the world—is a psychological necessity. Without it, you'd be paralyzed by every decision. You need to believe you're a reasonably competent person to function.

The problem is that this self-concept becomes a fortress. And any information that threatens it—any evidence that you're not as smart, not as capable, not as right as you thought—gets treated as an attack. Your brain doesn't process "you were wrong" as feedback. It processes it as a threat to your very identity. Neuroscience research has shown that the brain regions activated when our beliefs are challenged overlap significantly with the regions activated during physical pain. Being wrong literally hurts.

This is why arguments escalate. This is why people double down on bad positions. This is why a CEO who made a terrible strategic decision will restructure the entire company before admitting the decision was wrong. The ego would rather burn the building down than hand over the keys.

* * *

The Thanksgiving I Wasn't in the Stadium

I told a version of this story in another book, but it belongs here too, because it's the most vivid example I have of how ego makes you fail the people you love.

Thanksgiving, 2014. My first holiday with Izzy's extended family. Her aunt—let's call her Karen, because that's what she is—made a cruel comment about Izzy's weight in front of the whole table. Loud enough for everyone to hear. Designed to humiliate.

Izzy's eyes filled. The table went silent. And what did I do? Nothing. I sat there and stuffed mashed potatoes in my face because confrontation was uncomfortable and I didn't want to make things weird at a family dinner.

In the car afterward, Izzy said something I'll never forget: "You weren't even in the stadium." She explained: "When someone attacks me, I don't even need you to fight for me. Just be there. Show up. Let me know I'm not alone. But you were outside in the parking lot pretending nothing was happening."

She was right. And here's the ego connection: I didn't stay silent because I thought Karen was right. I stayed silent because speaking up would have made me uncomfortable. It would have disrupted my identity as the easygoing guy who gets along with everyone. My ego chose self-preservation over my wife's dignity. That's the ego problem in its most intimate, most damaging form—not in a boardroom or a laboratory, but at a dinner table with the person you love.

The next family gathering, Karen made another comment. This time, I was in the stadium. I said, calmly but clearly, "That's not okay. Don't talk to my wife that way." It was uncomfortable. Karen pitched a fit. And she never made another comment like that.

Ego wanted me to stay silent. Being an actual adult—or at least the closest I've ever come to one—required me to override it.

The Social Reinforcement Loop

It gets worse. Because ego doesn't operate in a vacuum. It operates in a social environment that constantly reinforces it.

Once you achieve a certain status—once you're the boss, the expert, the person with the title—the people around you start treating you differently. They laugh at your jokes even when they're not funny. They nod when you speak even when you're wrong. They stop challenging your ideas because challenging the boss is a career risk nobody wants to take at 9 a.m. on a Monday.

This creates what psychologists call a feedback vacuum. The higher you climb, the less honest feedback you receive, and the more confident you become in your own judgment—because nobody is telling you otherwise. You become increasingly certain that you're right about everything, precisely because the system has been designed to make sure no one tells you when you're wrong.

This is how "adults" are made. Not through wisdom, but through insulation. Every genius, executive, and leader we've profiled in Part II lived inside some version of this loop. Einstein's colleagues stopped challenging his rejection of quantum mechanics. Jobs's employees stopped questioning his medical choices. Blockbuster's board stopped questioning the business model. The loop doesn't create wisdom. It creates the feeling of wisdom. And the feeling is indistinguishable from the real thing—until it isn't.

Your Move: Override the Ego

The ego problem is the hardest one in this book to solve, because the ego is the one doing the solving. Asking your ego to fix itself is like asking the fox to redesign the henhouse security system.

But there are two things that work, and they're both uncomfortable:

First: build relationships with people who will tell you the truth. Not yes-people. Not sycophants. People like Izzy—people who love you enough to say, "You're wrong, and here's why," and mean it as a gift rather than an attack. These people are rare. They're invaluable. And your ego will try to drive them away, because honest feedback is the one thing ego can't survive.

Second: practice being wrong in low-stakes situations. Admit a small error publicly. Say "I was wrong about that" in a meeting when the stakes are low. Change your mind about something minor and announce it. Each time you do this, you're training your ego to tolerate the discomfort of being wrong—building the muscle that will let you admit bigger errors when the stakes are higher.

The ego will resist. It always does. But resistance is a signal, not a stop sign. When admitting you're wrong feels like dying, that's your ego talking. And your ego, as we've spent this entire book demonstrating, is not a reliable narrator. In the No-Adults Operating System, this is why Step 4 matters: check the incentives—including your own psychological incentive to be right.

So far, we've been focused on individual failure—single brains making single errors. But what happens when you put a roomful of those brains together, give them a budget and a mission, and call it a system? That's where things get truly terrifying.

Chapter 12: When the System Is the Problem

"No one raindrop believes it is responsible for the flood." —
Unknown

It Wasn't One Person. That's the Whole Problem.

Up to this point, we've been talking about individual adults who turned out to be spectacularly, entertainingly, sometimes catastrophically human. Einstein the bad husband. Newton the bubble investor. Jobs the carrot-juice oncologist.

Individual humans making individual mistakes because individual brains are riddled with cognitive biases and ego and the stubborn belief that being smart in one area makes you smart in all areas.

But here's where the book takes a darker turn. Because sometimes the problem isn't one person. Sometimes the problem is an entire system of adults—credentialed, experienced, well-intentioned adults—who collectively produce a disaster that none of them would have created alone. A system where every individual person can honestly say, "I was just doing my job," and they're not wrong, and people still end up dead.

This is where the thesis of this book gets truly frightening. Not that individual people are flawed—we've established that. But that the systems we build to compensate for individual flaws are themselves flawed in ways that nobody inside the system can see. The machine is broken, and every gear thinks it's working perfectly.

Welcome to institutional failure. Where the adults in the room aren't one person. They're the room itself.

Flint, Michigan: How Every Level of Government Poisoned a City and Shrugged

In April 2014, the city of Flint, Michigan, switched its drinking water supply from Detroit's system—sourced from Lake Huron, treated and tested for decades—to the Flint River. The reason? Cost savings. Flint was broke, and an unelected emergency manager appointed by the state governor decided that pumping water from a river that local residents had been swimming in, fishing from, and politely avoiding for years was the fiscally responsible move.

Almost immediately, residents complained. The water was discolored. It smelled wrong. It tasted wrong. People developed skin rashes, lost hair, and got sick. Parents noticed their children behaving differently. Something was obviously, viscerally wrong with the water.

The government's response, at every level, was a masterclass in institutional denial.

The city told residents the water was fine. The Michigan Department of Environmental Quality told residents the water was fine. When General Motors announced that the Flint River water was corroding newly machined engine parts at its local plant and switched to a different water source—because the water was too corrosive for car engines—the government still told residents the water was fine. For their bodies. Which are, you know, softer than engine parts.

Here's what actually happened: the Flint River water was highly corrosive. Properly treating it would have required adding anti-corrosion chemicals—a standard, well-understood process that costs roughly a hundred dollars a day. The emergency managers, whose expertise was in fiscal management and not in water chemistry, didn't authorize it. The state environmental regulators, who knew the treatment was required by federal law, told Flint's water plant that it wasn't necessary for a year. Without treatment, the corrosive water ate through Flint's aging lead pipes, and lead—a neurotoxin that causes permanent brain damage in children—leached into the drinking water of roughly a hundred thousand people.

Lead levels in some homes hit over a thousand parts per billion. The EPA's action level is fifteen.

Between six and fourteen thousand children were exposed.

The Anatomy of a System Failure

What makes Flint a case study in institutional failure—rather than just individual negligence—is the sheer number of adults who would have had to do their jobs correctly for this not to happen. And the sheer number of systems that would have had to function for the problem to be caught.

Start with the emergency manager. Michigan's emergency manager law gave an unelected appointee near-total control over the city's decisions. The manager's expertise was in fiscal policy, not public health, not water treatment, not environmental science. But the law gave him authority over all of those domains anyway. This is the Expertise Inversion from the last chapter, scaled up to a municipal government: the person with the authority to make the decision lacked the expertise to make it well, and the people with the expertise lacked the authority to stop him.

Then the state environmental regulators. The Michigan Department of Environmental Quality knew—or should have known—that switching to a corrosive water source without treatment violated federal law. They told the city otherwise. Not because they were evil, but because the institutional culture prioritized cost efficiency over precaution, because the people making the call were deferring to the emergency manager's authority, and because the system wasn't designed to escalate a problem that hadn't technically triggered the right regulatory box-check yet.

Then the EPA. A regional EPA manager named Miguel Del Toral flagged the lead contamination issue as early as April 2015—a full year after the water switch. He wrote an internal memo documenting the danger. The EPA sat on it. His own agency slow-walked the response, partly out of deference to the state regulators who were insisting everything was fine. The federal agency designed to catch exactly this kind of failure was deferring to the state agency that was causing it.

Then the elected officials. Flint's city council voted to reconnect to the Detroit water system. The emergency manager overruled them, calling the vote "incomprehensible." The democratic process that might have corrected the error was structurally powerless.

Then the governor's office. Communications later revealed that cost remained the central concern even as evidence of contamination mounted. The institutional incentive was to protect the emergency management framework—the governor's signature policy—not to protect the people it was supposed to serve.

Every single one of these actors can look at this sequence and say, with some justification, "I was operating within my authority. I followed the procedures. I deferred to the appropriate officials." And they'd be right. That's the terrifying part. The system worked exactly as designed. It just wasn't designed to protect people. It was designed to protect itself.

. . .

Normalization of Deviance: How "Good Enough" Becomes "Lethal"

After the Challenger disaster we discussed in the last chapter, sociologist Diane Vaughan coined a term that should be taught in every school and printed on every corporate conference room wall: normalization of deviance.

Here's how it works. An organization has a safety standard. Someone cuts a corner. Nothing bad happens. So the corner-cutting becomes the new normal. Then someone cuts another corner on top of that. Nothing bad happens. So that becomes the new normal. Each individual deviation is small, incremental, and seemingly harmless. And each time nothing goes wrong, the organization collectively confirms that the deviation is acceptable.

Until, eventually, the accumulated deviations reach a tipping point, and something catastrophic happens. And everyone in the organization says, "How could we have predicted this?" The answer is: you couldn't, because you were inside the system. Each step looked reasonable from where you were standing. The problem was the trajectory, and trajectories are invisible from the inside.

NASA's O-ring problem was a textbook case. Data showing O-ring erosion had existed since 1977. Every time a shuttle launched with minor erosion and didn't explode, the definition of "acceptable risk" expanded slightly. The engineers flagged it. Management acknowledged it. But because nothing had gone catastrophically wrong yet, the deviation was normalized. Each successful launch was treated as evidence that the risk was acceptable, rather than as evidence that they were getting lucky.

Flint's water crisis followed the same pattern. Regulatory corners had been cut for years—in water testing protocols, in enforcement timelines, in the treatment of financially distressed cities as problems to be managed rather than communities to be served. Each individual shortcut was small.

Each individual decision was defensible. And the cumulative result was that a hundred thousand people drank lead-contaminated water for eighteen months while every level of government told them it was fine.

Normalization of deviance is the institutional equivalent of the frog in boiling water. Except the frog is an entire population, and the water is literal.

The 2008 Financial Crisis: When the Smartest Room in the World Was the Dumbest

If Flint is what happens when a system fails the vulnerable, the 2008 financial crisis is what happens when a system fails everyone.

The basic story goes like this: American banks made enormous numbers of mortgage loans to people who couldn't afford them. They bundled those loans into complex financial products called mortgage-backed securities. Three credit rating agencies—Moody's, Standard & Poor's, and Fitch—gave those bundles their highest safety ratings, the coveted triple-A. Investors worldwide, including pension funds, municipalities, and retirement accounts for regular people, bought trillions of dollars worth of these products because the triple-A rating meant "virtually risk-free."

Then the housing market stopped going up. Borrowers defaulted. The securities collapsed. The global financial system imploded. Lehman Brothers—a one-hundred-and-sixty-year-old investment bank—filed the largest bankruptcy in American history. The U.S. government spent over seven hundred billion dollars bailing out financial institutions. Roughly eight million Americans lost their jobs. Millions lost their homes. The global economy contracted in ways that took nearly a decade to recover from.

And the question that everyone asks—that congressional commissions asked, that journalists asked, that laid-off workers and foreclosed families asked—is: how did nobody see this coming?

The answer is: some people did. But the system wasn't built to listen to them.

. . .

The Adults in the Room Were Paid Not to Notice

The Financial Crisis Inquiry Commission, established by Congress to investigate what went wrong, concluded that the three major credit rating agencies were "key enablers of the financial meltdown." They found that from 2000 to 2007, Moody's alone rated nearly forty-five thousand mortgage-related securities. Over half were given the triple-A rating. By April 2010, seventy-three percent of the mortgage-backed securities that Moody's had rated triple-A in 2006 had been downgraded to junk.

Seventy-three percent. Of the securities they had personally guaranteed were the safest investments on the planet.

How does that happen? Not through stupidity. The analysts at these agencies were genuinely smart. They had PhDs in mathematics and economics. They ran sophisticated models. They were, by any conventional definition, experts.

It happened because of a structural incentive that corrupted the entire system from the inside out. The rating agencies operated on an "issuer pays" model, meaning they were paid by the same banks whose securities they were rating. This is like a restaurant paying the health inspector directly and then being surprised when the inspection goes well. The agencies knew that if they gave tough ratings, the banks would simply take their business to a competitor. In the movie The Big Short, a character playing a Standard & Poor's employee explains why she keeps giving triple-A ratings to garbage securities: "If we don't give them the rating, they'll just go to Moody's."

So the analysts ran models that confirmed what their clients wanted to hear. The models were complex enough to look rigorous. The ratings were high enough to keep the fees flowing. And everyone in the system—the banks, the regulators, the investors, the agencies themselves—had an incentive to keep the machine running, because the machine was making everyone rich.

The adults in the room weren't incompetent. They were incentivized. The system wasn't broken. It was working exactly as designed. And the design was catastrophically misaligned with the public good.

. . .

The Diffusion of Responsibility: Why Nobody's Job Means Everybody's Problem

There's a psychological phenomenon called the bystander effect, and you've probably heard of it: the more people who witness an emergency, the less likely any individual person is to help, because everyone assumes someone else will step in. It's been studied extensively since the 1960s, and it explains why a person can collapse on a busy city street and nobody calls 911 for ten minutes.

Institutional failure runs on the organizational equivalent of the bystander effect. I call it the diffusion of responsibility, and it works like this: when a system has many people involved in a decision, each individual feels less personally responsible for the outcome. The emergency manager in Flint could point to the state regulators. The state regulators could point to the EPA. The EPA could point to the state. Everyone had a reasonable argument for why the failure was someone else's job to prevent.

In the financial crisis, the pattern was identical. The banks could point to the rating agencies—"they gave them triple-A."

The rating agencies could point to the banks—"they provided the data." The regulators could point to the complexity of the instruments—"nobody fully understood them." The investors could point to the ratings—"we trusted the experts."

Everyone was pointing at everyone else. And while they pointed, the system was collapsing.

The CEO of Citigroup told the Financial Crisis Inquiry Commission that a fifty-five-billion-dollar position in highly rated mortgage securities "would not in any way have excited my attention." The co-head of Citigroup's investment bank said he spent "a small fraction of one percent" of his time on those securities. Fifty-five billion dollars didn't excite anyone's attention because in a system that large, fifty-five billion was someone else's problem.

This is collective incompetence masquerading as distributed responsibility. Not because the individuals lacked capability, but because the system was designed so that no single person ever had to take full ownership of any single decision. Authority was distributed. Responsibility was diffused. And when the whole thing collapsed, no one person could be held accountable, because in a meaningful sense, no one person had made the decision. The system had made it, through a thousand small approvals, sign-offs, and unchallenged assumptions.

The system was the adult. And the system was guessing, just like everyone else.

The Collective Confidence Trap

Here's the pattern that connects Flint, the financial crisis, and the Challenger disaster. I call it the Collective Confidence Trap:

Step one: a group of credentialed adults are assembled to manage something important. Each individual is competent within their domain. Collectively, they project authority.

Step two: the system develops structural incentives that reward conformity, cost-cutting, or short-term results, and punish dissent, caution, or long-term thinking.

Step three: warning signs appear. Individuals within the system notice them. They raise concerns through the proper channels.

Step four: the system absorbs the warnings without changing course. The warnings are acknowledged, noted, filed, and functionally ignored—because the structural incentives haven't changed, and the people with the authority to change them are the same people who benefit from the status quo.

Step five: the disaster arrives. Everyone inside the system is shocked, because from where they were standing, everything was working.

Step six: investigations begin. Blame is distributed. Reports are written. Commissions are convened. Reforms are proposed. And the underlying structure—the incentive architecture, the authority distribution, the cultural norms that made the disaster possible—changes just enough to satisfy the public without actually threatening the system itself.

This is how institutional failure works. It's not that the adults in the room are bad people. It's that the room is designed wrong. And the people inside the room can't see the design, because the design is the water they're swimming in.

. . .

Why This Matters More Than Individual Failure

I could fill this entire book with individual adults who screwed up. In fact, that's what most books in this genre do. They tell you about the genius who made a dumb choice, the CEO who fumbled the future, the emperor who had no clothes. And those stories are useful. They're entertaining. They make us feel smart for recognizing what the genius missed.

But they also give us a comforting illusion: the illusion that the problem is individual. That if we could just replace the bad leader, hire the smarter CEO, elect the wiser politician, everything would work. The Great Person theory of history, except applied in reverse—the Great Screw-Up theory, where if you remove the one bad actor, the system hums along.

Institutional failure destroys that illusion. The Flint water crisis wasn't one bad actor. It was an entire chain of competent, credentialed adults operating within a system that was structurally incapable of protecting the people it was designed to serve. The 2008 financial crisis wasn't one rogue trader or one corrupt bank. It was a global financial architecture where the incentives pointed in the wrong direction and every institution followed them off a cliff, together, holding hands, in expensive suits.

The Challenger disaster wasn't one bad manager. It was an organizational culture where schedule pressure systematically overrode engineering judgment, and the procedures for raising safety concerns were no match for the procedures for getting a shuttle off the launch pad.

In each case, the adults existed. The expertise existed. The warnings existed. What didn't exist was a system designed to listen to its own people when they said something was wrong.

· · ·

A Personal Note on Systems

I work inside systems every day. I'm a corporate instructional designer, which means I build training programs within organizational structures that have their own incentives, their own blind spots, and their own normalization of deviance.

I've watched companies spend millions on training programs that teach employees the "right" way to do something while simultaneously maintaining incentive structures that reward the wrong way. I've seen safety training modules that are beautifully designed and completely ignored because the production floor rewards speed over caution. I've sat in meetings where everyone agreed that the current process was broken, and everyone left the meeting continuing to do it the broken way, because the system's momentum was stronger than any individual's desire to change it.

That's not because the people in those rooms were weak or stupid. It's because systems are powerful. They shape behavior more effectively than intentions, more reliably than willpower, and more stubbornly than good ideas. You can be the smartest person in the room and still be swept along by a current you can't even see.

This is why institutions fail just as reliably as individuals2014and often more catastrophically. We build systems hoping that the collective will be wiser than any single person. And sometimes it is. But sometimes the collective just becomes a bigger, more powerful, more confident version of the same flawed human judgment that got us into trouble in the first place—except now it has a budget, a legal team, and a communications department.

Your Move: Ask Structural Questions

Individual cognitive biases are hard enough to fight. Institutional ones feel damn near impossible. You can't exactly deprogram a bureaucracy or send an incentive structure to therapy.

But you can do this: start asking structural questions instead of personal ones.

When something goes wrong in an organization—a product fails, a patient is harmed, a policy backfires—the instinctive response is "who screwed up?" That's the individual-failure question. And it's the wrong question ninety percent of the time.

The better question is: what about this system made this outcome predictable? What incentives were in place? Who had the authority? Who had the expertise? Were those the same people? If someone saw this coming, why didn't the system respond? And who benefits from the system staying exactly the way it is?

These are uncomfortable questions, because they implicate the room, not just the person. They suggest that firing the CEO or prosecuting the manager might feel satisfying but won't actually fix the problem. They suggest that the problem might be structural, which means it might be expensive to fix, politically unpopular to fix, and resistant to the kind of quick, dramatic action that makes for good press conferences.

But they're the right questions. And asking them is, in its own quiet way, a form of actual adulthood.

Here's how to start building this muscle:

One: The next time you hear about a failure—a company scandal, a government blunder, a product recall—resist the urge to find a villain. Instead, ask: what was the incentive structure? Who was rewarded for what? Trace the incentives and you'll almost always find the cause.

Two: Look at your own workplace. Identify one area where what gets rewarded and what gets said are different. Does the company say "safety first" but reward speed? Does it say "innovation" but punish failure? Does it say "speak up" but promote the people who stay quiet? That gap between stated values and actual incentives is where institutional failure incubates.

Three: Ask yourself who the Roger Boisjoly is in your organization—the person with the data and the expertise who is being overruled by someone with the authority and the schedule pressure. If you can't identify that person, it might be because they've already been silenced. Or it might be because that person is you.

. . .

The children of Flint deserved adults who asked those questions before the water switch, not after. The families who lost their homes in 2008 deserved a financial system that asked those questions before the crash, not after. The crew of the Challenger deserved an organization that asked those questions before the launch, not after.

Individual humans are flawed. We've spent eight chapters establishing that. But the deeper, harder, more uncomfortable truth is that the systems we build to compensate for those individual flaws can be even more dangerous—because they aggregate our biases, insulate our egos, diffuse our responsibility, and normalize our deviations until the abnormal becomes routine and the routine becomes catastrophe.

Adults don't exist at the individual level. They don't exist at the institutional level either. But the institutions have bigger budgets and better PR.

So when someone tells you "the system works"—when they gesture at the credentials, the procedures, the oversight boards, the regulatory frameworks—remember Flint. Remember Challenger. Remember 2008. And ask the question that the system was never designed to answer:

"Works for whom?"

But they're the right questions. And asking them is, in its own quiet way, a form of actual adulthood. Not the kind that comes with a title or a corner office. The kind that comes from being willing to look at how things actually work instead of how they're supposed to work.

The children of Flint deserved adults who asked those questions before the water switch, not after. The families who lost their homes in 2008 deserved a financial system that asked those questions before the crash, not after. The crew of the Challenger deserved an organization that asked those questions before the launch, not after.

The adults didn't exist in time. But you're reading this now. Which means you have the chance to be the kind of person who asks the right questions before the disaster, even if the room doesn't want to hear them.

Especially if the room doesn't want to hear them.

Because that's usually when the questions matter most.

Chapter 13: The Algorithm Problem

The Pedestal Factory

Everything we've discussed in this book so far—the Confidence-Competence Gap, the halo effect, hero worship, the Illusion of Expertise, the Pedestal Economy—existed long before the internet. Humans have been confusing confidence for competence since the first cave person with a loud voice and a pointed stick convinced the rest of the group to follow them in the wrong direction.

But social media didn't just inherit these problems. It industrialized them.

What used to be a slow, local, person-to-person process—someone earns a reputation, people start listening to them, their influence grows within a community—has been replaced by a machine that can manufacture authority at scale, at speed, and with zero quality control. The Pedestal Economy used to be a farmers' market. Social media turned it into an Amazon warehouse, except the products are opinions and nobody checks what's in the box before shipping.

This chapter is about the machine itself: how social media algorithms work, what they're optimized for, and why they represent the single most powerful amplifier of false authority in human history.

. . .

What the Algorithm Actually Wants

Let's start with something that should be simple but isn't: social media algorithms are not designed to show you what's true. They are not designed to show you what's important. They are not designed to show you what's good for you, or for society, or for democracy, or for your blood pressure.

They are designed to do one thing: keep you on the platform as long as possible so you see more ads.

That's the business model. That's the whole thing. Every piece of content you see in your feed—every news story, every hot take, every inspirational quote, every angry rant—was served to you not because an editor decided it was important but because a mathematical model predicted it would keep you scrolling.

The metric that drives this system is called engagement. Engagement means any interaction: a like, a comment, a share, a hate-click, a rage-retweet, a screenshot sent to your group chat with the caption "can you believe this?" It doesn't matter whether the interaction is positive or negative, thoughtful or impulsive, informed or ignorant. The algorithm counts them all the same. A share is a share whether you're sharing because something is brilliant or because something is so catastrophically wrong that you can't believe another human being actually typed it.

And here's where it connects to everything in this book: research consistently shows that the content that generates the highest engagement is content that is emotionally provocative, morally outraged, and delivered with absolute confidence. Not content that is nuanced, accurate, or carefully qualified. Not content that says, "Well, it's complicated." Content that says, "THIS IS THE TRUTH AND EVERYONE ELSE IS AN IDIOT."

The algorithm doesn't know the difference between a Nobel laureate and a guy who once read a blog post. It only knows that one of them generates more engagement than the other. And the guy with the blog post and the unshakable confidence almost always wins.

The Confidence Economy on Steroids

Remember the Confidence-Competence Gap from Chapter 2? The principle that the less someone knows, the more confident they tend to be, while genuine experts tend to be cautious and qualified in their claims?

Social media algorithms have turned that gap into a canyon.

In the old media landscape, there were gatekeepers. You might disagree with how those gatekeepers operated—and there's plenty to criticize—but their existence meant that getting a platform required at least some minimum level of credibility. A newspaper editor had to agree to publish your opinion piece. A television producer had to agree to book you on their show. A publisher had to agree to print your book. Those gatekeepers were imperfect, biased, and often wrong. But they were a filter.

Social media removed the filter entirely.

Now, anyone can reach millions of people without any credential check, any editorial review, or any accountability mechanism whatsoever. The only qualification you need is the ability to generate engagement. And as we've established, the single most reliable way to generate engagement is to be confidently, emotionally, provocatively certain about things—regardless of whether you're right.

This means the algorithm systematically amplifies the Dunning-Kruger effect. The people who are most wrong but most confident get the biggest megaphones. The people who are most right but most careful get buried in the feed, because nuance doesn't go viral. "It's complicated" doesn't get shares. "Here are some things to consider" doesn't get likes. "I could be wrong about this" doesn't build a following.

What builds a following is certainty. And certainty, as we've spent twelve chapters demonstrating, is almost never earned.

• • •

The Outrage Engine

Researchers at Northwestern University published a study identifying the types of content that algorithms disproportionately amplify. They call it PRIME information: content that is Prestigious, Ingroup-affirming, Moral, and Emotional. In other words, content from people who look important, that confirms what your tribe already believes, that frames the issue in moral terms, and that makes you feel something—preferably something intense.

Notice what's not on that list: accuracy. Evidence. Nuance. Complexity. Self-correction.

The algorithm doesn't optimize for any of those things because none of those things reliably keep you scrolling. Accuracy is boring. Evidence is dense. Nuance is unshareable. Complexity requires effort. Self-correction makes you look weak.

What keeps you scrolling is outrage. Outrage is engagement gold. When you see something that makes you angry—a politician saying something infuriating, a celebrity making a terrible take, a stranger being confidently wrong in a way that personally offends you—your brain lights up. You engage. You comment. You quote-retweet with a snarky rebuttal. You send it to three friends. You spend forty-five minutes arguing with strangers about something that will matter to nobody in a week.

And the algorithm watches all of this and learns: that content works. Show more of it. Show it to similar users. Push it higher in the feed. Let it spread.

The result is what I call the Outrage Engine: a self-reinforcing cycle where confident, provocative, emotionally charged content generates engagement, which signals the algorithm to amplify it, which generates more engagement, which amplifies it further, until a random person's hot take about a topic they don't understand has reached more people than a carefully researched paper by an actual expert in the field.

The Outrage Engine doesn't just amplify bad information. It systematically disadvantages good information. It creates an information ecosystem where the loudest, angriest, most confident voice in the room gets the biggest platform—which is, if you'll recall, the exact opposite of what actually correlates with expertise.

The Manufacture of Authority

Here's where the algorithm problem intersects directly with the thesis of this book.

Social media doesn't just amplify confidence. It manufactures authority. And it does so through a mechanism that is invisible to most users: the follower count.

Think about how your brain processes a social media profile. You see a person's name, photo, bio, and follower count. If they have three hundred followers, your brain registers them as a regular person—someone with opinions but no particular authority. If they have three hundred thousand followers, your brain registers them differently. They seem important. Credible. Worth listening to. Their opinions feel more weighty, more significant, more likely to be correct.

But why? What does a large follower count actually tell you about a person's expertise? Absolutely nothing. A follower count tells you that a person has generated engagement. That's it. It tells you they said things that made people click. It doesn't tell you those things were true. It doesn't tell you they have credentials. It doesn't tell you they've ever been right about anything.

Yet our brains process follower counts as authority signals because we're running the same social-status software our ancestors used fifty thousand years ago. In a tribal environment, the person everybody listened to was probably the person worth listening to. Attention was a proxy for competence. The more people who deferred to someone, the more likely that someone had earned that deference.

On social media, that proxy is broken. Attention is no longer correlated with competence. It's correlated with engagement, which is correlated with emotional provocation, which is correlated with confidence, which is—as we've spent this entire book arguing—inversely correlated with actual expertise.

The algorithm has created a world where the people with the biggest platforms are systematically the people whose platforms are least deserved. Not always. But structurally, by design, as a default outcome of the system.

. . .

The Echo Chamber and the False Consensus

It gets worse. Because the algorithm doesn't just amplify confident voices. It also curates your entire information environment to confirm whatever you already believe.

This is the echo chamber effect, and it works like this: the algorithm notices that you engaged with a particular type of content—a political opinion, a health claim, a worldview. So it shows you more of that type of content. You engage with that, too, because it aligns with your existing beliefs (hello, confirmation bias). So the algorithm shows you even more. Over time, your feed becomes a mirror, reflecting your own views back at you from a hundred different angles, delivered by a hundred different confident voices who all seem to agree.

The result is a false consensus effect on steroids. You start to believe that "everyone" thinks the way you do, because everyone in your feed does. Opposing viewpoints become invisible—not because they don't exist, but because the algorithm filtered them out since showing them to you would reduce your engagement. The algorithm wants you happy and scrolling, not challenged and thinking. Discomfort is a bounce. Confirmation is a session.

This is catastrophic for the kind of thinking this book advocates. Everything we've talked about in Part IV— evaluating ideas on merit, seeking disconfirmation, questioning your own assumptions—requires exposure to viewpoints that challenge you. The algorithm does the opposite. It builds a comfortable, personalized information bubble where every confident voice agrees with you and the only thing that penetrates the bubble is outrage at the people outside it.

The algorithm doesn't build adults. It builds children with infinite access to people who tell them they're right.

Authority Laundering: How the Algorithm Creates Experts from Nothing

There's a process I've started calling authority laundering, and once you see it, you'll see it everywhere.

It works like this. A person posts a confident take on a topic. The algorithm amplifies it because it generates engagement. The post goes viral. Now the person has a large audience. Media outlets notice the person's large audience and invite them on television or quote them in articles. Now the person has media coverage. Other social media users see the media coverage and share it, saying, "This person is all over the news." The algorithm amplifies those shares. The audience grows further. Book publishers notice the growing audience and offer a book deal. Now the person has a book. Conferences notice the book and invite them to speak. Now they're a keynote speaker. The conference appearance gets posted to social media. The algorithm amplifies it. The cycle continues.

At no point in this process did anyone verify that the person was right about anything. At no point did anyone check their credentials, test their claims, or evaluate their track record. The entire authority-building process was driven by engagement metrics—by the algorithm's reward structure— and each step in the chain treated the previous step as evidence of legitimacy.

The follower count validated the media appearance. The media appearance validated the book deal. The book deal validated the speaking engagement. And the speaking engagement validated the follower count. It's a closed loop of manufactured authority, and the only input was the original algorithm boost.

This is how wellness influencers with no medical training end up with more health followers than most actual doctors. How finance bros with no fiduciary responsibility end up advising millions on their retirement savings. How parenting accounts run by twenty-three-year-olds without children end up shaping how actual parents raise their kids.

The algorithm laundered their attention into authority. And once the authority looks real—once the follower count is big enough, the media coverage is thick enough, the book deal is shiny enough—it becomes functionally indistinguishable from the real thing. Your brain can't tell the difference between earned authority and algorithmically manufactured authority, because the signals look identical.

* * *

The Speed Problem

There's one more dimension to the algorithm problem that makes it qualitatively different from anything humanity has dealt with before: speed.

In the pre-algorithm world, bad information spread slowly. A rumor might travel through a village in a day, a city in a week, a country in a month. At each step, there were opportunities for correction. Someone who knew better could push back. An editor could fact-check. A trusted voice could say, "Wait, that's not right." The information traveled at human speed through human networks, and the correction mechanisms operated at roughly the same speed.

Algorithms destroyed that balance. False information now spreads globally in hours. Corrections, when they arrive, reach a fraction of the audience that saw the original claim. A study published in Science found that false news stories on Twitter reached fifteen hundred people six times faster than true stories, and true stories rarely reached more than a thousand people at all. Falsehood is faster because it's more surprising, more emotional, more engaging—exactly the qualities the algorithm rewards.

This means the algorithm doesn't just give an unfair advantage to confident people over cautious ones. It gives an unfair advantage to fast-and-wrong over slow-and-right. The expert who takes a day to carefully evaluate the evidence and produce a nuanced take is structurally disadvantaged against the person who immediately fires off a confident opinion within five minutes of the news breaking. By the time the careful analysis arrives, the narrative has already been set. The confident first-mover has defined the conversation. The correction is always playing catch-up, and it almost never catches up.

This is the epistemological crisis of our time. Not that people are stupid—they're not. Not that information is unavailable—it's everywhere. But that the distribution system for information systematically favors speed and confidence over accuracy and care. The most wrong person in the room gets the fastest megaphone. The most right person in the room shows up after the audience has already left.

• • •

An Izzy Moment

My wife Izzy is one of the smartest people I know, and she has a fraction of the social media following of people who are confidently wrong about topics she actually understands. She runs a professional handywoman business across multiple cities. She knows construction, repair, building codes, and how things actually work in the physical world. She has real expertise, built through real work, tested against real outcomes.

And she watches, regularly, as DIY influencers with massive followings post home repair advice that is not just wrong but actively dangerous. Electrical work that violates code. Load-bearing wall modifications that could collapse a structure. Plumbing shortcuts that will cause water damage in six months. These posts get millions of views because they're edited beautifully, delivered confidently, and set to upbeat music.

Izzy once showed me a video that had twelve million views and said, "If someone actually does this, their bathroom is going to flood." I asked why she didn't make a response video. She said, "Because 'actually, this is more complicated than it looks' doesn't get twelve million views. 'Watch me do this in thirty seconds' does."

She's right. And that's the entire algorithm problem in one sentence. Expertise is complicated, cautious, and qualified. The algorithm rewards simple, confident, and fast. The incentive structure of social media is fundamentally incompatible with the kind of careful, honest, domain-specific expertise that actually helps people.

Izzy still posts her real expertise. She still does the work. But the algorithm isn't built to find her. It's built to find the person who makes the dangerous thing look easy.

The Doomscroll Confession

I'm going to come clean about something, because this chapter doesn't work if I pretend I'm above any of this. I doomscroll. I do. I'm an instructional designer with three master's degrees and a bookshelf full of books about cognitive biases, and I still find myself, at eleven-thirty at night, thumbing through my phone, consuming content that is making me angrier and less informed with every swipe. I know how the algorithm works. I've literally written about how the algorithm works. And it still gets me.

Because that's the point. The algorithm isn't designed to be defeated by knowledge. It's designed to exploit the same emotional circuitry that keeps us watching car accidents, arguing with strangers, and eating the second slice of cake we didn't need. Knowing the trick doesn't make you immune to it. It just makes you frustrated with yourself while you keep falling for it.

I wrote about this in another book—the insidious pull of the infinite scroll, the way algorithms learn your vulnerabilities faster than you can build defenses against them. And the conclusion I came to there is the same one I'll give you here: the answer is not willpower. The answer is architecture. You have to change the structure of your information diet the same way you'd change the structure of your kitchen if you wanted to eat healthier. Don't rely on discipline when you can redesign the environment.

Why This Is the Biggest Threat to Thinking for Yourself

Every chapter in this book has been building toward a single idea: think for yourself. Don't outsource your judgment to confident-sounding people. Don't trust the pedestal. Evaluate ideas on merit. Practice intellectual humility.

The algorithm is the single biggest obstacle to all of that.

Not because it's malicious. The engineers who build these systems aren't trying to make you stupid. They're trying to keep you engaged, which is their job, because engagement is how their company makes money. The problem isn't evil intent. The problem is structural incentive misalignment—the same pattern we identified in the Flint water crisis, the 2008 financial crash, and the Challenger disaster. The system is working as designed. The design just happens to be catastrophically bad for human cognition.

Social media platforms are, in their current form, Pedestal Factories. They mass-produce false authority. They systematically reward confidence over competence. They filter out complexity and nuance. They exploit cognitive biases that we've spent this entire book identifying. And they do it twenty-four hours a day, seven days a week, in your pocket, on the device you check a hundred and fifty times a day.

This is not a problem you can think your way out of while the firehose is pointed at your face.

. . .

Your Move: Build Early Warning Systems

The structural solutions to this problem—changing how algorithms rank content, requiring transparency from platforms, building regulation that aligns engagement incentives with public good—are important, necessary, and largely outside your individual control. So let's focus on what is within your control.

One: Audit your information diet. Right now. Open your phone and look at who you follow and what you've engaged with in the last week. Ask yourself: how many of these people are experts in the things they're talking about? How many of them got into my feed because they said something accurate versus something that made me feel something? How many of them have I ever seen say, "I was wrong about this"? If the answers are uncomfortable, good. That's the audit working.

Two: Deliberately follow people who challenge you. Not trolls. Not people who make you angry for the sake of anger. People who are thoughtful, credentialed in their actual domain, and willing to say things you disagree with. The algorithm will fight you on this—it wants to keep you comfortable. Override it. Seek out the voices that make you think, not just the ones that make you nod.

Three: Set structural limits. Time limits. App limits. Phone-in-another-room limits. The algorithm is a better manipulator than you are a resister, so don't try to out-willpower it. Change the architecture. Make doomscrolling harder. Make reading a book easier. Make the healthy choice the default choice. You're an instructional designer's reader now; you know that environment shapes behavior more than intentions do.

Four: When you see a confident claim on social media that generates a strong emotional reaction in you, treat that reaction as a warning signal, not a validation. The strength of your emotional response is not evidence that the claim is true.

It is evidence that the claim was engineered—by the poster or by the algorithm—to generate exactly that response. Pause. Check. Verify. And if you can't verify it in thirty seconds, don't share it. The world will survive without your retweet.

. . .

The Pedestal Economy has always existed. Humans have always confused confidence with competence, attention with authority, popularity with truth. That's hardwired.

But for most of human history, the Pedestal Economy operated at human speed, in human-sized communities, with human-scale consequences. If a village elder gave bad advice, the village learned. If a newspaper got a story wrong, the correction ran on page seven the next day. If a pundit was consistently wrong, their audience slowly drifted away.

The algorithm eliminated all of those corrective mechanisms and replaced them with a system that optimizes for the exact opposite of truth: emotional engagement. The correction never runs. The audience never drifts away. The confident-but-wrong person never loses their platform, because being wrong doesn't reduce engagement. Often, it increases it.

We are living in the first era of human history where the Pedestal Economy operates at machine speed, at global scale, with no editorial filter, no correction mechanism, and no incentive to be right.

Every cognitive bias we've catalogued in this book—every halo effect, every Dunning-Kruger spiral, every confirmation bias feedback loop—is being exploited and amplified by a machine that processes billions of interactions per day and optimizes relentlessly for the metric that correlates least with truth: emotional engagement.

The algorithm didn't create the Pedestal Economy. Humans built that on their own, over millennia, one misplaced trust at a time. But the algorithm supercharged it. It took a human tendency and gave it the processing power of a data center. It took a cognitive vulnerability and turned it into a business model. It took the gap between confidence and competence and turned it into an expressway.

Adults have never existed. But the machine that manufactures fake ones has never been this efficient.

Keep that in mind next time you open your phone. The algorithm has opinions about who you should trust. And the algorithm, like every other authority we've examined in this book, is guessing.

It just guesses faster than you can think.

And that speed advantage is why everything in Part IV of this book—the frameworks, the exercises, the thinking tools— matters more now than it ever would have in any previous era. Because you're not just fighting your own cognitive biases anymore. You're fighting your cognitive biases plus a trillion- dollar machine that has mapped those biases and exploits them for profit. The fight isn't fair. But knowing the fight exists is the first step toward not losing it by default.

And for the record: the fact that you're reading a book right now instead of scrolling? That's already a small victory. The algorithm wanted you on your phone tonight. You're here instead. That counts for more than you think.

Chapter 14: How Smart People Get Manipulated

*"The most effective way to destroy
people is to deny and obliterate their
own understanding of their history."*
— George Orwell

You're Not Too Smart to Be Fooled. You're Smart Enough to Fool Yourself.

We've spent the last several chapters cataloging the ways your brain lies to you. Cognitive biases. Ego protection. Institutional incentives. Algorithmic manipulation. All the invisible machinery humming away beneath the surface of your conscious mind, nudging your beliefs and decisions in directions you didn't choose.

But here's the part nobody wants to hear: everything we've discussed so far happens to you naturally. These are bugs in your cognitive software—unintentional, automatic, evolved features that helped your ancestors survive but occasionally misfire in the modern world.

This chapter is about something worse. This chapter is about the people who know about those bugs and use them on purpose.

Not hackers. Not criminals. Not shadowy conspirators in underground bunkers. I'm talking about advertisers, politicians, media companies, influencers, corporations, and anyone else who has studied the map of human cognitive weakness and decided to use it as a business plan.

Because here's the uncomfortable truth that connects everything in this book: if you understand how cognitive biases work, you can exploit them. And smart people—the very people who think they're immune to manipulation—are often the easiest targets. Because intelligence gives you better tools for rationalizing why you fell for it.

. . .

The Illusory Truth Effect: How Repetition Becomes Reality

In 1977, researchers at Villanova and Temple Universities made a discovery so simple and so devastating that it should be printed on every classroom wall, every newsroom whiteboard, and every social media loading screen in the world.

They found that if you tell people a statement twice, they're more likely to believe it's true—even if it's false. Even if they knew it was false the first time they heard it.

This is the illusory truth effect, and it is, without exaggeration, the foundational principle of propaganda, advertising, and political messaging.

Here's how it works. Your brain has a shortcut for evaluating whether something is true: Does it feel familiar? Familiar information is processed more fluently—your brain recognizes it, retrieves it faster, and that fluency creates a subjective feeling of "rightness." Your brain doesn't tag the source of that familiarity. It doesn't say, "This feels familiar because you heard it on a podcast, and that podcast was wrong." It just says, "This feels familiar, therefore it's probably true."

Repetition creates familiarity. Familiarity creates fluency. Fluency feels like truth. That's the entire mechanism. Three steps from lie to belief, and your conscious mind never gets a vote.

And it gets worse. Subsequent research has shown that the illusory truth effect works even when the repeated statement contradicts things you actually know. In studies at Vanderbilt University, participants who correctly answered a trivia question and demonstrably knew the right answer still rated the false version as more true after hearing it repeated. Prior knowledge did not protect them. Being right did not protect them. Intelligence did not protect them.

Monetary incentives for accuracy didn't protect them. Warning labels that said "disputed by third-party fact-checkers" didn't protect them. Even explicitly labeling the source as unreliable didn't eliminate the effect.

Let that sink in. The most basic defense you think you have— knowing the truth—does not fully protect you from believing a lie you've heard enough times. Your brain's truth-detection system runs on familiarity, and familiarity is hackable by anyone with a message and the patience to repeat it.

Every advertiser knows this. Every political strategist knows this. Every propagandist in history has known this, even before the science put a name on it. If you say something often enough, people will believe it. Not because they're stupid. Because their brains are working exactly as designed—and the design has a vulnerability that anyone can exploit.

. . .

The Framing Effect: How the Same Truth Can Make You Choose Differently

In 1981, psychologists Daniel Kahneman and Amos Tversky presented research participants with a scenario: six hundred people are about to die from a disease. You must choose between two treatment programs.

Half the participants got the options framed in terms of lives saved. Program A: two hundred people will be saved for certain. Program B: a one-in-three chance that all six hundred will be saved, and a two-in-three chance that nobody will be saved.

The other half got the exact same options, framed in terms of deaths. Program C: four hundred people will die for certain. Program D: a one-in-three chance that nobody dies, and a two-in-three chance that all six hundred die.

143

Programs A and C are identical. Programs B and D are identical. The outcomes are mathematically equivalent. The only thing that changed was the words.

And yet seventy-two percent of people chose Program A when it was framed as "two hundred saved," while only twenty-two percent chose Program C when the identical outcome was framed as "four hundred will die." Same outcome. Different frame. Completely reversed preference.

This is the framing effect, and it's one of the most replicated findings in the history of psychology. How you describe a choice changes which choice people make—even when the options are objectively identical. Your brain doesn't evaluate the raw data. It evaluates the story the data is wrapped in.

Now think about how many decisions you make every day that have been framed for you by someone else. The politician who says "tax relief" instead of "tax cuts for corporations." The doctor who says "ninety percent survival rate" instead of "ten percent chance of death." The salesperson who says "save three hundred dollars" instead of "spend twelve hundred dollars."

Every one of those framings is a choice someone made about how to present information to you. And every one of them nudges your decision in a direction the framer intended. Not because they're lying—often the information is technically accurate—but because they're exploiting a cognitive vulnerability that makes you respond to packaging as if it were content.

The frame is never neutral. The frame is always a choice. And the person who chose it usually has an agenda.

The Semmelweis Reflex: Why We Reject What Threatens Us

We met Ignaz Semmelweis earlier in this book—the doctor who discovered that hand-washing could save mothers' lives and was destroyed by the medical establishment for saying so. His story gave rise to a named cognitive phenomenon: the Semmelweis Reflex, the automatic tendency to reject new information that contradicts established beliefs, norms, or identity.

But I want to take this concept further than the historical anecdote, because the Semmelweis Reflex isn't just something that happened to nineteenth-century doctors. It's something that happens to you, every day, and it's one of the primary mechanisms through which smart people get manipulated.

Here's how it works as a manipulation tool: if someone wants to protect a false belief—whether it's a product claim, a political narrative, or a corporate talking point—they don't have to prove the belief is true. They just have to make the contradicting evidence feel threatening to your identity.

If you've built your professional identity around a particular approach, and someone presents evidence that the approach is flawed, your Semmelweis Reflex will kick in before your rational mind even has time to evaluate the evidence. The information feels like an attack on who you are, so your brain rejects it reflexively—not because it's wrong, but because accepting it would cost you something.

Manipulators exploit this by framing challenges to their position as attacks on your tribe, your values, or your intelligence. "If you believe the experts on this, you're just a sheep." "They're trying to take away your freedom." "The establishment doesn't want you to know this." These framings don't engage your analytical mind. They engage your identity-defense system. And once your identity is on the line, evidence becomes irrelevant. You're no longer evaluating a claim. You're defending yourself.

This is how entire populations can be convinced to reject scientific consensus, medical evidence, or economic data—not through better arguments, but through identity hijacking. The manipulator doesn't need to out-think you. They just need to make the truth feel like it belongs to the enemy.

The Anchoring Exploit

We covered anchoring in an earlier chapter as a cognitive bias—the tendency to fixate on the first piece of information you encounter. But I want you to see it now through the lens of deliberate exploitation, because anchoring isn't just something that happens to you accidentally. It's something people do to you on purpose.

Every negotiation trainer teaches anchoring as a strategy. Whoever puts the first number on the table controls the conversation, because everyone else's brain will anchor to that number regardless of whether it's reasonable. This is why car salespeople start high. Why retailers show the "original price" crossed out next to the "sale price." Why consultants quote a premium package before showing you the standard option.

But anchoring goes far beyond sales. Political campaigns anchor you to extreme positions so that their actual position seems moderate by comparison. Media outlets anchor you to the most dramatic interpretation of events so that the slightly-less-dramatic truth seems comforting. Thought leaders anchor you to their framework before you've had time to develop your own, so everything you encounter afterward gets evaluated through their lens.

The anchor doesn't have to be accurate. It doesn't even have to be plausible. Research shows that even obviously arbitrary anchors—like asking people to spin a wheel of fortune before estimating a number—influence subsequent judgments. Your brain grabs the first number it encounters and uses it as a reference point, regardless of where that number came from.

Every time someone presents you with information in a particular order, they're anchoring you. And you almost never notice, because the anchor operates below the threshold of conscious awareness. By the time you're evaluating the options, the frame has already been set.

* * *

Social Proof: The Exploitation of "Everybody Thinks So"

There's a reason laugh tracks exist on sitcoms. Not because television executives think you're too stupid to know when something is funny, but because research consistently shows that when you hear other people laughing, you're more likely to laugh yourself. The laughter of strangers makes the jokes seem funnier. Not logically—the joke didn't change—but perceptually. Your brain uses the reactions of other people as data about reality.

This is social proof, and it's one of the most powerful influence mechanisms ever documented. We use other people's behavior as a shortcut for figuring out what's correct, what's safe, and what's normal. In most situations, this works reasonably well. If a restaurant is packed, the food is probably decent. If everyone is evacuating a building, you should probably evacuate too. Social proof is an efficient heuristic for navigating a complex social world.

148

But when social proof is manufactured—when the crowd reaction is fake, purchased, or algorithmically inflated—it becomes one of the most effective manipulation tools available.

Fake reviews. Purchased followers. Astroturfing campaigns where a small number of operatives create the illusion of widespread public support. Bot networks that amplify a message until it appears to be a grassroots movement. Testimonials from paid actors. Comments sections filled with sock puppet accounts. All of these are techniques for manufacturing social proof—for making it look like "everybody thinks so" when in reality, nobody does.

And your brain can't tell the difference. It processes manufactured consensus the same way it processes real consensus. If it looks like a lot of people believe something, your brain nudges you toward believing it too—regardless of whether those "people" are real, informed, or even human.

This is particularly dangerous in combination with the algorithm problem we discussed in the last chapter. Social media platforms amplify content based on engagement, and manufactured social proof generates engagement. So the algorithm boosts the artificially popular content, which generates real engagement from real people, which generates more amplification, and within hours, a manufactured consensus has become an actual one. The initial lie has been laundered into truth through the machinery of social proof and algorithmic amplification.

Every time you make a decision because "everyone seems to agree," ask yourself: how do I know everyone agrees? Did I independently verify that? Or did I see a number on a screen and let my brain do the rest?

· · ·

The Weaponization of Trust

Everything we've talked about in this chapter converges on a single point: the exploitation of trust.

The entire thesis of this book is that we place too much trust in authority, confidence, and credentials—that we outsource our judgment to people we've never vetted because they look like they know what they're doing. And every manipulation tactic we've examined in this chapter is, at its core, a method for manufacturing or hijacking that trust.

Repetition creates trust. If something feels familiar, it feels trustworthy. Framing creates trust. If something is presented in the right language, with the right emotional valence, it feels trustworthy. Identity hijacking creates trust. If someone positions themselves on your side of the tribal line, they feel trustworthy. Anchoring creates trust. If someone establishes the baseline for comparison, everything they say afterward feels reasonable.

None of these trust signals have anything to do with whether the person is actually correct, actually competent, or actually acting in your interest. They're all hacks—exploits that target the same cognitive shortcuts your brain uses to navigate a complex world quickly. And they work on smart people just as well as anyone else. Sometimes better, because smart people are better at constructing post-hoc rationalizations for why they fell for it.

• • •

A Confession That Still Stings

I'll tell you about the time I got manipulated, because this chapter is dishonest if I don't.

Years ago, early in my corporate career, I had a boss who was extraordinarily charismatic. The kind of person who could walk into a room and make everyone feel like they were the most important person in it. He had confidence. He had presence. He had the title. And he had a plan for our department that he presented with such conviction, such clarity, such intellectual authority that I bought in completely. I didn't just support the plan. I championed it. I defended it in meetings. I pushed back on colleagues who raised concerns.

The plan failed. Spectacularly. Not because of bad luck or unforeseeable circumstances, but because the core assumptions were wrong—and several people had tried to point that out early on. People I had dismissed. People I had

151

argued with. People whose objections I had written off as resistance to change.

I wasn't stupid. I was smart. That was the problem. My intelligence gave me the tools to construct elaborate justifications for a position I'd adopted not because of evidence but because of charisma. I had been anchored by my boss's confidence. I had been framed by his narrative. I had experienced the Semmelweis Reflex against the very people trying to correct course. And I had rationalized all of it as "strategic thinking."

That failure taught me something I still carry: the smarter you are, the more sophisticated your rationalizations become. Intelligence doesn't protect you from manipulation. It just upgrades the quality of your excuses after the fact.

* * *

The Manipulation Stack

Here's the thing that makes all of this so dangerous: these techniques don't operate in isolation. They stack. A skilled manipulator—whether a propagandist, a marketer, or a cult leader—uses multiple techniques simultaneously, each one reinforcing the others.

The illusory truth effect provides the baseline: repeat the message until it feels familiar. Framing controls the interpretation: present the message in a way that triggers the desired emotional response. Identity hijacking prevents questioning: position anyone who disagrees as an outsider, an enemy, or a fool. Anchoring sets the terms: establish the boundaries of the conversation so that even the "moderate" position is one you've chosen. Social proof provides validation: surround the message with confident voices who agree.

Stack all of these together, and you get a manipulation system that is almost impossible to resist in real time. Not because you're weak, but because each layer exploits a different cognitive vulnerability, and you don't have enough conscious attention to monitor all of them simultaneously. It's like trying to play defense in basketball while being attacked from five directions at once.

This is why "just think critically" is inadequate advice. Critical thinking is a conscious, effortful process. Manipulation targets unconscious, effortless processes. By the time your critical thinking kicks in, the anchor is set, the frame is established, the familiar-feeling message has already registered as "probably true," and your identity is engaged in defending the position. You're not thinking critically at that point. You're performing critical thinking on behalf of a conclusion you've already been nudged toward.

. . .

Manipulation in Everyday Life: It's Not Just the Big Stuff

I want to make sure this chapter doesn't leave you thinking manipulation is only something that happens in political campaigns and advertising boardrooms. It happens in your daily life, in mundane settings, from people who aren't trying to be manipulative but are using these techniques because they work.

Your doctor frames your treatment options in a way that nudges you toward the choice they prefer. Your boss anchors salary conversations to numbers that benefit the company. Your kids—if you have them—learn social proof manipulation before they can tie their shoes ("But everyone else gets to stay up late!"). Your friends use repetition to normalize their preferences ("We should really try that restaurant" said fourteen times becomes an irresistible suggestion). Your partner frames household responsibilities in ways that make their contribution seem larger and yours seem smaller, or vice versa.

None of this is sinister. It's human. We are all, always, framing, anchoring, and using social proof—usually without conscious intent. The question isn't whether these dynamics exist in your relationships and your workplace. The question is whether you're aware of them.

Because awareness is the only defense. Not immunity—awareness. The moment you notice a frame, you've already weakened its power. The moment you identify an anchor, you can consciously adjust away from it. The moment you ask "who actually agrees with this, and how do I know?" you've broken the spell of social proof.

You can't stop being manipulated. But you can get faster at noticing when it's happening. And that speed—the gap between the manipulation hitting and your awareness catching up—is the margin where free will lives.

How I Use This (Imperfectly)

You can't immunize yourself against manipulation. I need you to accept that upfront. Anyone who tells you they're too smart to be manipulated is someone who is currently being manipulated and doesn't know it. The cognitive vulnerabilities these techniques exploit are hardwired. You can't uninstall them.

But you can build early warning systems. Here's how:

One: Watch for repetition without evidence. If someone's argument relies on saying the same thing louder and more often rather than presenting new evidence, that's the illusory truth effect being deployed. The strength of a claim is not determined by how many times you've heard it. It's determined by the evidence supporting it. If the evidence isn't growing but the repetition is, someone is trying to make familiarity do the work that facts couldn't.

Two: Identify the frame before evaluating the content. When someone presents you with a choice, ask: "How else could this be described?" If a politician says "job-killing regulation," reframe it as "environmental protection measure" and see if your reaction changes. If it does, you were responding to the frame, not the policy.

Three: Notice when disagreement feels personal. If someone challenges a belief and your first instinct is defensiveness rather than curiosity—if you feel attacked rather than informed—that's your Semmelweis Reflex firing. Pause. Ask yourself: am I rejecting this because it's wrong, or because accepting it would change something about how I see myself?

Four: Seek out the anchor. In any negotiation, any pitch, any presentation—ask: what's the first number or claim that was put in front of me, and who put it there? That anchor is shaping everything else I'm evaluating. What would I think if I'd encountered a different first number?

Five: Distrust your own rationalizations. This is the hardest one, and it's the most important. If you find yourself constructing an elaborate explanation for why you believe something, ask: did I arrive at this belief through evidence, or did I arrive at the evidence through the belief? Smart people build beautiful logical structures on rotten foundations all the time. The structure feels solid. The foundation is vibes.

· · ·

We started this book by dismantling the myth of the competent authority2014showing that nobody has it figured out, that even the smartest people are improvising. This chapter adds a darker layer: not only are we all guessing, but there are entire industries built on exploiting the way we guess.

The advertising industry. The political consulting industry. The social media attention economy. The wellness-industrial complex. The self-help grift. These are not conspiracy theories. These are business models. They work because human cognitive vulnerabilities are predictable, exploitable, and profitable.

And the best defense against them is not intelligence. It's not education. It's not credentials. It's the willingness to say, out loud, to yourself, on a regular basis: "I can be fooled. I have been fooled. And the fact that I'm smart doesn't make me harder to fool—it makes me better at not noticing."

That sentence is the beginning of real protection. Not because it makes you invulnerable, but because it keeps you vigilant. And in a world full of confident guessing, sophisticated manipulation, and algorithmic amplification, vigilance is the closest thing to a superpower any of us will ever have.

The adults don't exist. The manipulators know it. They know that your brain is running on ancient software with known vulnerabilities. They know that your confidence in your own judgment is itself a vulnerability. They know that the smarter you feel, the less likely you are to question whether your beliefs arrived through evidence or through exploitation.

The only advantage you have is knowing what they know. Not to become paranoid—paranoia is just another cognitive bias wearing a trench coat. But to become aware. To develop the habit of pausing between stimulus and response, between hearing a claim and believing it, between feeling certain and acting on that certainty.

That pause is everything. It's where the manipulation fails. It's where the frame gets noticed. It's where the repetition gets flagged. It's where the anchor gets identified. It's where you stop being a consumer of someone else's narrative and start being the author of your own.

Use it.

Chapter 15: The Beautiful Mess of Being Human

Why Failure Isn't the Opposite of Success—It's the Ingredient

Okay. Deep breath.

We've spent fourteen chapters systematically dismantling the idea that anyone has it figured out. We've dragged geniuses off their pedestals. We've exposed the cognitive biases that warp every brain on the planet. We've documented how institutions fail, how algorithms exploit, and how smart people get manipulated by systems designed to hack their own psychology. We've established, with considerable evidence and what I hope was at least some entertainment value, that the human brain is basically a well-meaning liar with a flair for the dramatic.

If you're feeling a little demoralized right now, I understand. That's a lot of demolition. It's like watching someone take a wrecking ball to a building you've been living in your whole life—the building called "somebody knows what they're doing."

Now it's time for the good news.

Because here's the thing about discovering that adults don't exist: it's not a tragedy. It's a liberation.

The Permission You Didn't Know You Needed

If nobody has it figured out, then you don't have to have it figured out either.

Read that again. Let it settle.

That pressure you've been carrying—the feeling that everyone else seems to know what they're doing and you're the only one faking it—you can put it down now. It was always an illusion. Everyone is faking it. The CEO is faking it with better suits. The doctor is faking it with better vocabulary. The professor is faking it with better footnotes. The parent is faking it with better snacks. Everyone is navigating uncertainty with incomplete information and hoping like hell they get it mostly right.

And most of the time? They do get it mostly right. Not because they're adults. Because they're humans who keep showing up, keep adjusting, and keep stumbling forward despite not having a map.

That's not failure. That's the whole game.

• • •

The Science of Bouncing

There's a body of research in psychology on what's called post-traumatic growth—the documented phenomenon where people who go through difficult, even devastating experiences don't just recover to their baseline but actually grow beyond it.

Psychologists Richard Tedeschi and Lawrence Calhoun first described it in the mid-1990s, and since then it's been documented across hundreds of studies: people who experience serious illness, loss, trauma, or failure frequently report that the experience changed them in positive ways—deeper relationships, greater appreciation for life, revised priorities, a stronger sense of personal strength they didn't know they had.

This isn't toxic positivity. It's not "everything happens for a reason." Sometimes terrible things happen for no reason at all, and pretending otherwise is insulting. What post-traumatic growth shows is something more nuanced: that humans have an extraordinary capacity to make meaning from suffering, to build new structures on the rubble of old ones, to emerge from the worst chapters of their lives with capabilities they wouldn't have developed any other way.

Not because suffering is good. Because humans are resilient in ways that our culture of confident authority-worship completely fails to acknowledge. We're told to look for answers in experts, leaders, and systems. But the most powerful engine of growth isn't external authority. It's the internal process of falling, hurting, learning, and rebuilding.

. . .

2017: The Year Everything Broke

I need to get personal here, because this chapter doesn't work as theory. It only works as testimony.

In August 2017, my mom had a stroke. A thousand miles away. Meanwhile, my wife Izzy was having thirty to forty seizures a day and needed me there. So what do I do? Abandon my wife to be with my mom? Stay with my wife and leave my mom to handle this alone? Neither option felt good. Neither option was right. There was no adult to call, no authority to consult, no framework that could resolve the impossible math of being needed in two places at once.

My sister—who had a strained relationship with our mom for years—stepped up. She took care of her. They reconnected. Something that had been broken for decades began to heal, precisely because I couldn't be there.

Then Hurricane Irma ripped through my home.

Then Izzy had brain tumor surgery.

Then—two weeks later—Izzy felt better than she had in years.

It was chaos. It was awful. And every single disaster had something hidden in it that I couldn't see at the time but can see now.

I'm not telling you this to be inspirational. I'm telling you because it's the most honest proof I have that the thesis of this book isn't just intellectual. In the worst year of my life, there were no adults. Not the doctors, who were guessing with better instruments. Not the insurance adjusters, who were following scripts. Not me, who was supposed to be the steady one and was instead a terrified man making impossible decisions with no manual and no time.

And we survived. Not because someone knew what they were doing. Because everyone kept going when nobody knew what they were doing. That's what humans do. Not adults. Humans.

. . .

Famous Humans Who Kept Going

Michael Jordan was cut from his high school basketball team. The most famous basketball player in history wasn't good enough to make varsity as a sophomore. He later said he went home, closed his bedroom door, and cried. Then he spent the summer working harder than he'd ever worked in his life. The failure didn't motivate him because failure is inherently motivating—it isn't. He chose to use it as fuel. That choice was the thing. Not the talent. The choice.

Colonel Harland Sanders was rejected over a thousand times before someone agreed to franchise his fried chicken recipe. He was in his sixties. He'd failed at everything else he'd tried—law, insurance, tire sales, a ferry boat company, a motel. The man was a walking catalogue of unsuccessful ventures. And he became the face of a global fast-food empire because he kept knocking on doors when any reasonable "adult" would have retired to a porch rocker and accepted defeat.

James Dyson built five thousand one hundred and twenty-seven failed prototypes before his vacuum cleaner worked. He spent fifteen years and his entire savings on something that didn't exist yet, running on nothing but the belief that the next attempt might be the one. Not certainty. Belief. There's a difference. Certainty is what the Pedestal Economy sells. Belief is what the actual humans in this book ran on.

Steven Spielberg was rejected multiple times by the University of Southern California's film school. The most commercially successful director in cinema history wasn't good enough for film school, according to the adults who evaluated his application.

Dr. Seuss—born Theodore Geisel—had his first manuscript rejected by twenty-eight publishers. Twenty-eight adults whose professional expertise was identifying children's literature that would sell looked at the work of the most beloved children's author in American history and said no.

· · ·

The Pattern Behind the Pattern

These stories aren't about grit or hustle or any of the other buzzwords that get slapped on motivational posters and sold as coffee mugs. They're about something far more fundamental: the willingness to be wrong, to fail, to look foolish, and to keep going anyway.

But here's what I want you to notice—something that connects these stories to every other chapter in this book: in every single case, the "adults" were wrong. The coaches who cut Jordan. The investors who rejected Sanders. The publishers who passed on Dr. Seuss. The admissions officers who refused Spielberg. These weren't random strangers guessing blindly. They were credentialed professionals applying their expertise to a specific evaluation—and getting it catastrophically wrong.

The system evaluated these people and rendered its verdict. And the verdict was wrong. Because the system is made of people. And people—as we've spent fourteen chapters demonstrating with exhausting thoroughness—are working with incomplete information, cognitive biases, and the stubborn belief that being experienced makes you infallible.

The beautiful mess of being human isn't just that we fail. It's that we fail, and the people judging us fail at evaluating our failures, and the systems built to help us fail at catching the failures of the people judging us, and somehow, despite all of this cascading imperfection, some of us build vacuum cleaners that work on attempt five thousand one hundred and twenty-eight.

That's not a system working. That's a species refusing to stop. And it's the most hopeful thing I know.

* * *

The Pivot

So here's where the book changes gears.

Part I told you the lie: adults exist. Part II showed you the evidence: they don't. Part III explained the machinery: here's why.

Part IV is going to give you the tools to do something about it.

Not a guru to follow. Not a pedestal to build. Not a system to trust blindly. But a set of thinking tools—practical, testable, usable—that work regardless of who's using them, that correct for the biases we've cataloged, and that produce better decisions over time even when the decision-maker is flawed.

Which, as we've established, is always.

You're not going to become an adult in Part IV. Nobody is. But you might become something better: a human who has stopped waiting for the adults to show up and started building the tools to navigate the uncertainty yourself.

That's not something adults do. That's something humans do when they stop pretending they're supposed to be adults.

Let's build.

PART IV

BUILDING SOMETHING BETTER

"The measure of intelligence is the ability to change." — Albert Einstein (who, as we've discussed, had his own issues)

Chapter 16: Stop Following People. Start Evaluating Ideas.

The First Rule of Thinking for Yourself

If the central thesis of this book is that adults don't exist—that no one has a monopoly on wisdom and that authority is more often performed than earned—then the obvious follow-up question is: "So what do I do instead?"

The answer is deceptively simple and incredibly hard to practice: stop evaluating people and start evaluating ideas.

. . .

We've been trained since birth to assess the messenger before the message. Is this person credible? Do they have the right title? The right degree? The right number of followers? The right outfit? If the messenger checks enough boxes, we accept the message without much scrutiny.

This is backwards. And it's the source of most of the problems we've explored in this book.

The CEO who crashes a company wasn't followed because of their ideas. They were followed because they were the CEO. The doctor who dismisses your symptoms isn't trusted because of their diagnostic reasoning in that specific moment. They're trusted because they have "MD" after their name. The influencer who sells you a supplement isn't persuasive because of the evidence. They're persuasive because they have abs and good lighting.

The Idea Evaluation Framework

Here's a simple framework you can use any time someone—anyone—presents you with a claim, a plan, or an opinion:

First: What is the evidence? Not "who said it" or "how confidently did they say it," but what actual evidence supports this claim? Is there data? Is it peer-reviewed? Can it be independently verified? If the answer to all three is no, what you're looking at is an opinion dressed up as a fact. That's fine—opinions have value—but don't confuse the costume for the content.

Second: What are the counterarguments? Every idea has weaknesses. If the person presenting the idea can't articulate the strongest argument against it, they haven't thought about it enough. And if you can't articulate the counterargument either, neither have you. This is the steelmanning principle from Chapter 19—don't fight the weak version of the opposing view. Engage the strong one.

Third: What does this person have to gain? This isn't about being cynical. It's about being realistic. A pharmaceutical company promoting its own drug has a different incentive structure than an independent researcher evaluating the same drug. A real estate agent telling you "now is a great time to buy" gets a commission if you do. A consultant recommending more consulting gets more billable hours. Both might be right. But the incentives matter, and pretending they don't is how you end up on the wrong end of someone else's business model.

Fourth: Would I believe this if it came from someone I don't respect? This is the killer question. If your favorite thought leader said it, you'd nod along. But if that guy from high school who eats paste said the exact same thing, would you still agree? If the answer is no, you're following a person, not evaluating an idea. The truth value of a claim doesn't change based on who's delivering it. Either the evidence is there or it isn't.

. . .

How I Use This (Imperfectly)

I'll be honest: I don't run this framework on every claim I encounter. Nobody does. If I evaluated every statement I heard with full rigor, I'd never make it through a grocery run. The framework is for decisions that matter—health decisions, financial decisions, career decisions, decisions about who to trust with your time, money, or attention.

Where I've found it most useful is in meetings. I spent years in corporate environments where the highest-paid person's opinion automatically became the strategy. The Idea

Evaluation Framework gave me a way to separate the opinion from the title. "Interesting. What's the evidence for that?" is a complete, polite, professional sentence that accomplishes more intellectual work than an hour of nodding.

Try it once. Just once. The next time someone with a big title says something with big confidence, ask: "What evidence supports that?" Watch what happens. Either they'll have evidence—in which case you've learned something—or they won't, in which case you've learned something even more valuable.

Chapter 17: How to Detect False Authority

A Survival Guide for the Pedestal Economy

We live in an age of unprecedented access to information and, simultaneously, unprecedented access to misinformation. Everyone has a platform. Everyone has an audience. And as we explored in Chapter 13, the algorithms that power social media don't care about accuracy—they care about engagement. Confident nonsense is more engaging than careful truth, which means the Pedestal Economy has never been more powerful or more dangerous.

So how do you navigate it? How do you tell the difference between genuine authority and the performance of authority?

. . .

Red Flags of False Authority

They have credentials in one field but speak with authority in another. This is the Illusion of Expertise from Chapter 4 in its most common form. A brilliant physicist is not automatically a reliable source on nutrition, economics, or public policy. A successful entrepreneur is not automatically qualified to redesign the education system. Excellence in one domain does not transfer to expertise in all domains, no matter how much the halo effect wants you to believe otherwise.

They cannot explain their reasoning in plain language. Real experts can simplify complex ideas without losing accuracy. Richard Feynman, one of the greatest physicists of the twentieth century, was famous for his ability to explain quantum mechanics to undergraduates. If someone needs jargon to sound credible, they might be hiding the fact that they don't fully understand what they're saying. Complexity is not a credential. Clarity is.

They never say "I don't know." This is the biggest red flag of all. The most knowledgeable people in any field are acutely aware of the boundaries of their knowledge. When an expert says "I don't know" or "the evidence is mixed," that's a sign of genuine competence, not weakness. Anyone who has an answer for everything has examined nothing.

They respond to questions with deflection or aggression. "How dare you question me" is not an answer. It's a defense mechanism. It's the sound of someone whose authority is based on the pedestal, not the evidence. Every expert in this book who was catastrophically wrong—the Thiokol managers, the Decca Records executive, the doctors who rejected Semmelweis—responded to challenges with some version of "how dare you." The pattern is consistent enough to be a diagnostic tool.

They have a financial incentive to believe what they're saying. The supplement guru selling the supplements. The consultant recommending more consulting. The author telling you this book will change your life. (I make no such promises. Buy snacks instead. The snacks will definitely change your life, at least for the next twenty minutes.)

. . .

Green Flags of Genuine Expertise

They welcome scrutiny. Real experts know that challenges make ideas better, not weaker. If someone invites you to poke holes in their argument, they've probably already poked most of them themselves.

They distinguish between what they know and what they believe. There's a huge difference between "the evidence shows" and "I think." Genuine experts are careful about which one they're offering. When they slip into opinion, they flag it.

They change their minds when presented with new evidence. This is the gold standard. If someone has publicly updated their position based on new data, they are practicing intellectual honesty—Bayesian updating in action—and you should trust them more, not less.

They can steelman the opposing view. If an expert can articulate the best possible version of the argument against their own position, it means they've genuinely engaged with the complexity. If they can only strawman the opposition, they're performing authority, not practicing it.

. . .

The One-Minute Authority Audit

Here's a practical tool you can run in sixty seconds. The next time someone is trying to persuade you of something—a talking head, a colleague, an influencer, a politician, an author—run through three questions:

One: Is their expertise in this specific topic? Not "are they smart" or "are they successful." This topic. This claim. This domain.

Two: Can I find someone with equal credentials who disagrees? If yes, the issue is more complex than one person's confidence suggests, and you need to evaluate the evidence, not the people.

Three: What happens to them if I believe them? Do they get money, followers, votes, clicks, or validation? If yes, raise your evidence bar. Not because incentives make people wrong, but because incentives make people persuasive regardless of whether they're right.

Three questions. Sixty seconds. It won't make you infallible. But it'll cut your vulnerability to false authority in half. And in the Pedestal Economy, cutting your vulnerability in half is a competitive advantage that most people don't have. This One-Minute Authority Audit is a condensed version of the No-Adults Operating System's first four steps—and in the next two chapters, you'll get the full toolkit.

Chapter 18: Think in Probabilities, Not Certainties

How to Be Confidently Uncertain

One of the most destructive habits in human thinking is the addiction to certainty. We want clear answers. We want yes or no, right or wrong, black or white. We want someone to tell us what's going to happen, and we want them to be sure about it.

This is a child's way of thinking. And I don't mean that as an insult. Children need certainty because the world is overwhelming and they don't have the tools to process ambiguity. "Is this safe?" "Is this person good or bad?" These binary questions serve a survival function when you're five. But you're not five anymore. And the world is not binary.

● ● ●

The Umbrella Principle

Probabilistic thinking is the practice of assigning likelihoods to outcomes instead of committing to one prediction. It sounds technical, but you already do it in low-stakes situations. When you check the weather forecast and it says seventy percent chance of rain, you bring an umbrella but don't cancel your plans. You're thinking probabilistically. You're holding two possibilities in your mind simultaneously—

it might rain, it might not—and making a decision that accounts for both.

Now imagine applying that same approach to everything else. Instead of "The stock market will go up," try "There's a sixty percent chance it goes up, a thirty percent chance it stays flat, and a ten percent chance it drops significantly." Instead of "This diet will work," try "There's good evidence this approach helps most people, but individual results vary, and I should track my own data." Instead of "This candidate will be great for the job," try "Based on the interviews and references, I'd say seventy percent chance of success, with the main risk being that they struggle with the pace."

This isn't wishy-washy fence-sitting. It's intellectual honesty. It's acknowledging that the world is complex and that our predictions are educated guesses, not divine prophecies. And it's the single most effective defense against the overconfidence effect we identified in Chapter 2.

Why Certainty Is Dangerous

Every catastrophic failure in this book was driven, at some level, by false certainty. Chamberlain was certain he could negotiate with Hitler. Blockbuster was certain people would always want physical stores. The rating agencies were certain their models accurately priced risk. Thiokol's managers were certain the data was inconclusive. Elizabeth Holmes was certain her technology would eventually work.

None of them said, "There's a thirty percent chance I'm wrong about this, so let me build a contingency." If they had, the outcomes might have been very different. Probabilistic thinkers build contingencies. Certainty addicts don't, because building a contingency means admitting you might need one, and that feels like weakness.

It's not weakness. It's wisdom. The difference between a good pilot and a dead one is that the good pilot always has an alternate airport in mind. Not because they expect to need it. Because they know they might.

The Beauty of "I Might Be Wrong"

"I might be wrong" is not a weakness. It's a superpower. It's the four-word phrase that separates people who learn from people who stagnate. It's the antidote to the ego problem we explored in Chapter 11.

When you say "I might be wrong," you open a door. You create space for new information, for correction, for growth. When you insist you're right, you slam that door shut and brick it over and pretend the room behind it doesn't exist.

The most successful people in every field—the ones who actually earn their pedestals—are the ones who practice this relentlessly. Scientists who say "the data suggests" instead of "I know." Entrepreneurs who say "let's test that" instead of "my gut says." Leaders who say "What am I missing?" instead of "What are they missing?"

These are not adults. They're humans who have made peace with uncertainty and learned to navigate it instead of pretending it doesn't exist.

Your Move: Start Assigning Probabilities

Start small. The next time someone asks for your opinion on something uncertain—a prediction, a plan, a recommendation—attach a probability. Not in your head. Out loud. "I'm about seventy percent confident this will work." "I'd say there's maybe a forty percent chance that's accurate."

Two things will happen. First, people will look at you strangely, because nobody talks like this. Second, you will immediately start making better decisions, because the act of assigning a number forces you to honestly assess how much you actually know. And once you start tracking your predictions, you'll discover—as every calibration study has shown—that you're less accurate than you think you are. Which is humbling. And which is the entire point.

Chapter 19: The Skill of Thinking

"It is the mark of an educated mind to be able to entertain a thought without accepting it." — Aristotle

Thinking Is Not Something You're Born With. It's Something You Build.

We've spent twenty chapters dismantling the myth that adults exist—that somewhere out there, somebody has it figured out. We've looked at geniuses who stumbled, institutions that failed, algorithms that exploit, and manipulators who weaponize your own brain against you. If I've done my job, you're now thoroughly convinced that nobody—not the expert, not the CEO, not the influencer, not the guy with three master's degrees writing this book—has a monopoly on truth.

So now what?

If you can't trust people, and you can't trust institutions, and you can't even fully trust your own brain—what's left?

Process. That's what's left.

Not a person to follow. Not a guru to trust. Not a credential to hide behind. A process—a set of thinking tools that work regardless of who's using them, that correct for the biases we've cataloged, and that produce better decisions over time even when the decision-maker is flawed. Which, as we've established, is always.

This chapter is where the instructional designer in me takes over. I've spent decades building learning systems that teach adults how to think more clearly, make better decisions, and catch their own cognitive mistakes before those mistakes become expensive. Now I'm going to teach you the same thing.

Fair warning: this is the most tool-heavy chapter in the book. It's going to feel different from the rest. More practical, less snarky. That's intentional. The snark got you in the door. The tools are why you stay.

. . .

Tool 1: Bayesian Updating (or, How to Change Your Mind Like a Grown-Up)

The single most important thinking skill you can develop is the ability to update your beliefs when you encounter new evidence. This sounds simple. It is not. As we've discussed at length, your brain is designed to protect existing beliefs, not revise them. Cognitive dissonance, confirmation bias, the Semmelweis Reflex—all of these conspire to keep your current beliefs intact, regardless of what the evidence says.

Bayesian thinking is the antidote. Named after Thomas Bayes, an eighteenth-century Presbyterian minister and mathematician (because of course the solution to modern epistemic chaos was invented by a clergyman doing math on the side), Bayesian updating is a formal framework for adjusting your confidence in a belief based on new evidence.

181

Here's the simplified version, stripped of all the math that would make your eyes glaze over:

Step one: Before you encounter new evidence, you have a prior belief—your current best guess about how likely something is to be true. Maybe you're seventy percent confident that a particular diet is healthy, or sixty percent confident that a business strategy will work. The specific number matters less than the act of assigning one, because putting a number on your confidence forces you to admit that you're not certain. And admitting uncertainty is the first step toward being updatable.

Step two: You encounter new evidence. A study comes out. A prediction is tested. New data arrives. The question is: does this evidence change how confident you should be?

Step three: You update. Not to one hundred percent or zero percent, but incrementally. If the evidence supports your belief, your confidence goes up a little. If it contradicts your belief, your confidence goes down a little. The key word is proportionally—strong evidence should move your confidence more than weak evidence. A well-designed randomized controlled trial should move your confidence more than your friend's anecdote. A pattern across multiple studies should move your confidence more than a single result.

Step four: You repeat this process continuously. Your beliefs are never fixed. They're living, breathing estimates that get refined every time you encounter relevant information.

This sounds mechanical, and in its formal mathematical version, it is. But in practice, you don't need the math. You just need the mindset. Every time you encounter new information about a belief you hold, ask yourself: Does this change what I think? If so, by how much? And is my adjustment proportional to the quality of the evidence, or am I dismissing strong evidence because it contradicts my current position?

The most common failure mode is asymmetric updating: people adjust their confidence upward easily when evidence confirms their belief, but refuse to adjust it downward when evidence contradicts it. If you catch yourself doing this—if you eagerly accept confirming evidence but explain away disconfirming evidence—you're not thinking. You're defending.

Bayesian updating doesn't require you to be right. It requires you to be honest about how confident you are and willing to change when the evidence changes. That's it. And that alone will put you ahead of approximately ninety percent of public discourse.

Here's what Bayesian thinking looks like in practice. You read an article claiming that a new supplement improves memory. Your prior: you're maybe twenty percent confident, because most supplement claims don't hold up. You check the evidence: it's a single study, small sample, funded by the supplement company. Your confidence stays at twenty percent. Maybe drops to fifteen. You see three more articles repeating the claim—but they all cite the same single study. Your confidence doesn't change, because repetition of the same evidence is not new evidence. Then a large independent meta-analysis comes out showing no effect. Your confidence drops to five percent. You don't buy the supplement. Your friend, who heard the claim four times and never checked the source, is currently on his third bottle. That's the difference Bayesian thinking makes.

* * *

Tool 2: The Pre-Mortem (or, How to Fail Before You Start)

In the late 1990s, psychologist Gary Klein developed a technique so simple, so effective, and so contrary to how most organizations operate that it should be standard practice in every boardroom, classroom, and household on the planet. He called it the pre-mortem.

Here's how it works. You're about to make a decision—launch a project, commit to a strategy, make a major purchase, take a new job, whatever. Before you proceed, you do this exercise: imagine that it's one year from now, and the decision has failed catastrophically. Not just didn't work out. Failed. Spectacularly. Now ask yourself: why?

That's it. That's the whole technique. Imagine the failure has already happened, and then generate reasons for it.

It sounds too simple to be powerful. It isn't. Research from Wharton, Cornell, and the University of Colorado found that this approach—what scientists call "prospective hindsight"—increases the ability to accurately identify reasons for future outcomes by thirty percent compared to standard forward-looking risk assessment.

Why does it work so much better than just asking "what could go wrong?"? Because of the cognitive shift. When you ask people what could go wrong with a plan they're excited about, their brain's ego-protection machinery kicks in. They minimize risks. They explain away concerns. They don't want to be the buzzkill. The social pressure to be supportive overwhelms the analytical pressure to be honest.

But when you tell them the project has already failed—when failure is presented as a certainty rather than a possibility—the dynamic flips. Now people aren't undermining the plan. They're explaining what happened. They're showing how smart they are by identifying the failure points that nobody else saw. The psychological safety reverses: instead of feeling like a troublemaker for raising concerns, you feel like the sharpest person in the room.

Daniel Kahneman—the Nobel Prize-winning psychologist whose work appears throughout this book—has publicly endorsed the pre-mortem as one of the most effective debiasing techniques available. In his book Thinking, Fast and

Slow, he recommends it specifically as a tool for combating the planning fallacy and optimism bias.

I use pre-mortems in my instructional design work constantly. Before I launch a training program, I sit with the team and say, "It's six months from now. This program has completely flopped. Nobody completed it. The client is furious. Why?" And every single time, someone says something nobody had considered. Every single time, the exercise surfaces a risk that standard planning missed.

You can use this for anything. A career change. A relationship decision. A financial commitment. A health plan. Before you commit, mentally fast-forward to the failure and work backward. The future version of you who made this decision and regretted it—what would they say went wrong?

Listen to that version of yourself. They're smarter than you think.

Tool 3: The Decision Journal (or, How to Stop Lying to Your Future Self)

Here's a question that will make you uncomfortable: how do you know your past decisions were good or bad?

Most people evaluate their decisions based on outcomes. If the decision led to a good result, it was a good decision. If it led to a bad result, it was a bad decision. This seems logical. It is not.

186

It is one of the most common and most damaging thinking errors in human cognition, and it has a name: outcome bias.

A decision can be excellent—well-reasoned, based on the best available evidence, appropriately calibrated for uncertainty—and still produce a bad outcome because the world is uncertain and some percentage of good decisions will, by chance, fail. Conversely, a decision can be terrible—reckless, poorly informed, based on ego and vibes—and still produce a good outcome because sometimes you get lucky.

If you only evaluate decisions by their outcomes, you'll learn the wrong lessons. You'll repeat bad processes that happened to work. You'll abandon good processes that happened to fail. Over time, your decision-making will get worse, not better, because your feedback loop is broken.

The fix is a decision journal. And it's embarrassingly simple. Before you make any significant decision, write down the following: What is the decision? What are the alternatives I considered? What evidence supports each option? What is my confidence level (as a percentage) that this will work? What are the key assumptions I'm making? What would change my mind?

That's the entry. It takes five minutes. Then you go make the decision and live your life.

Six months later, or a year later, or whenever the outcome becomes clear, you go back and read the entry. Not to judge yourself—to learn. Was your confidence level calibrated? Did the outcome match your prediction? Were your assumptions correct? If not, which ones failed? Was there evidence available at the time that you ignored?

Over time, patterns emerge. You discover that you're consistently overconfident about certain types of decisions. Or that you systematically underweight certain kinds of evidence. Or that your best decisions happen when you consult specific people, and your worst happen when you rush. The journal becomes a map of your cognitive tendencies—not the generic cognitive biases from a psychology textbook, but your specific, personal patterns of error.

Nobody does this. Almost nobody. And the reason nobody does it is the same reason most people never audit their own track record: we2019d rather believe we're good decision-makers than prove it. The journal would force us to confront the gap between how good we think we are and how good we actually are. And most people would rather not know.

Be the person who wants to know.

. . .

Tool 4: Steelmanning (or, How to Win Arguments by Losing Them First)

You've probably heard of a strawman argument—taking your opponent's position, weakening it into a version they didn't actually argue, and then triumphantly defeating the weakened version. It's the debating equivalent of beating up a scarecrow and claiming you won a boxing match.

Steelmanning is the opposite. It's the practice of taking your opponent's position and making it as strong as possible before you respond to it. Not the weak version. Not the dumb version. Not the version that's easy to dismiss. The best, most charitable, most defensible version of the argument you disagree with.

Why would you do this? Isn't the point of an argument to win? No. The point of thinking is to be right. And you cannot know whether you're right unless you've genuinely engaged with the strongest version of the opposing view. If you can only defeat the weak version of a counterargument, you haven't proven your position is strong. You've proven you're good at picking easy fights.

In practice, steelmanning works like this. Someone disagrees with you. Before you respond, pause and ask yourself: What is the strongest version of their argument? What evidence would support their position? What would a reasonable, intelligent person need to believe for this position to make sense? If you can't answer those questions, you don't understand the disagreement well enough to have a useful opinion about it.

Steelmanning has a side benefit that's almost more valuable than the thinking improvement: it completely changes the dynamic of disagreements. When you demonstrate that you understand someone's position better than they've articulated it—when you say, "If I understand correctly, the strongest version of your point is this—am I getting that right?"—they immediately become more receptive to your response. Because you've shown them the rarest thing in modern discourse: genuine engagement with their actual ideas, not a caricature designed to make them look stupid.

This is the instructional designer in me talking: the best way to change someone's mind is not to attack their weakest argument. It's to demonstrate that you've understood their strongest argument and still have a better one. That's not winning. That's teaching. And teaching is how actual adults—if they existed—would handle disagreement.

Tool 5: The No-Adults Operating System

Now let me tie all of these tools together into something you can actually use in the wild. I call it the No-Adults Operating System, and it's a six-step process you can run anytime you're confronted with a claim, a decision, or a confident voice telling you what to think.

Step one: Pause. Before you react emotionally, buy yourself three seconds. That's all you need. Three seconds is the gap between your brain's automatic System 1 response and your deliberate System 2 analysis. In those three seconds, you go from being a passenger to being a driver. Emotional reactions are not evidence. They're reflexes. Treat them as data about yourself, not data about the claim.

Step two: Identify the claim. What, specifically, is being asserted? Not the emotional wrapper. Not the confidence of the person delivering it. Not the number of people who seem to agree. The actual claim. Strip it naked and look at it without the packaging.

Step three: Check the evidence. What evidence supports this claim? Is it peer-reviewed? Has it been replicated? Is it anecdotal or systematic? Is the person presenting evidence, or just presenting confidence? Remember: the strength of someone's conviction is not evidence for the truth of their claim. Passion is not proof.

Step four: Check the incentives. What does the person making this claim have to gain from you believing it? Are they selling something? Running for office? Building a platform? Protecting their reputation? This isn't cynicism—it's realism. Incentives don't make someone wrong, but they do mean you should require stronger evidence before believing them.

Step five: Assign a probability. Don't commit to "true" or "false." Commit to a likelihood. "I'm about sixty percent confident this is accurate" is infinitely more honest and useful than "This is definitely true." Probabilities force humility. They leave room for updating. They prevent the kind of all-or-nothing commitment that makes you resistant to new evidence.

Step six: Pre-mortem the decision. If I act on this belief and I'm wrong, what happens? What's the cost? Is it reversible? The higher the stakes and the less reversible the consequences, the higher your evidence bar should be. You can afford to be wrong about what restaurant to try. You cannot afford to be wrong about your retirement savings or your medical treatment.

Six steps. Pause. Identify. Evidence. Incentives. Probability. Pre-mortem. You can run this process in thirty seconds for low-stakes decisions and in thirty minutes for life-changing ones. The steps don't change. Only the depth of your analysis does.

. . .

A Worked Example: The Operating System in Action

Let me show you what this looks like in practice, using a real scenario from my own life.

A few years ago, a colleague at work—someone I respected, someone with a big title and a track record—pitched me on a side business opportunity. He was confident. He had numbers. He had testimonials. He had that energy that makes you feel like you're being invited into something exclusive. Everything about the presentation triggered my brain's "this person is credible, follow them" subroutine.

Old me would have said yes on the spot. Post-book me ran the Operating System.

Pause. I noticed I was excited, which is an emotional state, not an analytical one. Excitement is the feeling that says "jump" before your brain has finished calculating how far down it is.

Identify. The core claim was: invest this amount, follow this model, and you'll see this return within this timeframe. Stripped of the charisma and the PowerPoint, it was a financial prediction from a single source with no independent verification.

Evidence. I asked for documentation. Third-party audits. Verifiable track records. He had testimonials—which are social proof, not evidence. He had projections—which are predictions, not data. The actual evidence base was thin.

Incentives. He earned a commission on every person he recruited. His financial incentive was for me to say yes regardless of whether the opportunity was sound. That didn't make him dishonest. But it meant I needed a higher evidence bar.

Probability. Based on the evidence available, I assigned maybe a thirty percent chance that the returns were realistic. Possible? Sure. Probable? No. And the downside risk—losing the investment entirely—was a hundred percent possibility with real financial consequences.

Pre-mortem. I imagined it was a year from now and I'd lost the money. What would I say went wrong? "I trusted a confident person instead of verifying the numbers. I let social pressure override due diligence. I made a financial decision based on a feeling." All of which, as this entire book argues, is exactly how adults fail.

I passed. He was surprised. He was a little offended. And six months later, the opportunity collapsed exactly the way my pre-mortem predicted.

I'm not telling you this story to seem smart. I'm telling you because the Operating System is the only reason I didn't make the same mistake I've made a dozen times before. Left to my instincts—left to my brain's default settings—I would have followed the confident person with the nice presentation. The tools caught what my intuition missed.

. . .

Tool 6: The Disagreement Protocol

One more tool, because it addresses the scenario where most of these thinking skills collapse: the moment someone disagrees with you and your ego catches fire.

Here's the protocol. When someone challenges your position and you feel the heat rising in your chest, run through these four questions before you respond:

First: What specifically are they claiming? Not "they're attacking me." What is the specific factual or logical claim they're making? Separate the claim from the emotion.

Second: Is there any evidence that supports their position? Even if you disagree, even if it makes you uncomfortable—is there anything in what they're saying that might be right? If you can't find a single grain of truth in an opposing view, you probably haven't looked hard enough.

Third: What would it cost me to be wrong? Not socially—forget your ego for a second. What would it actually cost me, in real-world consequences, to update my position? Usually, the cost is much lower than your ego is telling you it is.

Fourth: Am I defending my position because of evidence, or because changing my mind would feel like losing? If the answer is the latter, you're not thinking. You're fighting. And fighting is not a thinking skill. It's an ego skill. They're different.

My wife Izzy is the best disagreement partner I've ever had, precisely because she doesn't let me get away with ego-defense disguised as logic. She has this way of cutting through my elaborate rationalizations with a single sentence that makes me realize I'm not actually arguing a point—I'm just refusing to lose. "You're not defending an idea right now," she'll say. "You're defending your ego. Stop it."

Find an Izzy. Protect that relationship. The person who tells you when you're wrong—not to hurt you, but because they

love you enough to prioritize your growth over your comfort—
is the most valuable person in your life.

. . .

Why This Chapter Exists

I'm aware that a chapter full of thinking frameworks in a book
that's mostly funny stories about geniuses screwing up might
feel like a gear change. It is. Intentionally.

Because the funny stories are the diagnosis. They're the part of
the doctor's visit where you find out what's wrong. This
chapter is the prescription. And prescriptions aren't as fun as
diagnoses, but they're considerably more useful.

Every person we've profiled in this book—Einstein, Newton,
Edison, Jobs, the executives at Blockbuster, the managers at
Thiokol, the regulators in Flint—could have benefited from
these tools. Not because the tools are magic, but because they
externalize the thinking process. They take the decision out of
your head, where your biases live, and put it on paper, where
you can actually see it.

That externalization is the whole game. You cannot debug
software while it's running. You have to stop, look at the code,
identify the bug, and fix it. Your brain is software. These tools
are the debugger.

The Humility Clause

One last thing. And this matters enough that I'm going to say it directly, without the usual snark.

These tools will make you a better thinker. They will not make you a perfect thinker. There is no such thing. Every tool has limitations. Bayesian updating requires you to accurately assess evidence quality, and humans are bad at that. Pre-mortems can identify risks but not all risks. Decision journals only work if you're honest in them. Steelmanning requires you to genuinely engage with opposing views, which your ego will resist at every turn.

The goal is not perfection. The goal is better. Better than yesterday. Better than your default. Better than the version of you that makes decisions on autopilot and evaluates them through the lens of ego and hindsight.

If you use these tools even inconsistently—if you run the No-Adults Operating System even half the time—you will make better decisions than most of the adults we've profiled in this book. Not because you're smarter than Einstein or Steve Jobs. But because you're willing to do something they often weren't: build a process that's stronger than your instincts.

That's not adulthood. That's better than adulthood. That's what you build when you stop pretending the adults will save you and start building the tools to save yourself.

I teach these tools for a living. I've taught them in Fortune 500 boardrooms and small team meetings and over coffee with friends who were about to make terrible decisions. And the single most common thing I hear after someone actually uses them for the first time is some version of: "Why didn't anyone teach me this in school?"

The answer is depressing but honest: because school was designed to teach you what to think, not how to think. It was designed to produce obedient citizens who could pass standardized tests, not independent thinkers who could evaluate claims, detect manipulation, and update their beliefs when the evidence changed. The system that was supposed to produce adults produced people who are very good at memorizing answers and very bad at questioning whether the answers are right.

This book can't fix the education system. But it can give you six tools that the education system never did. And if you use them—imperfectly, inconsistently, humanly—you'll be better equipped to navigate a world full of confident guessing than any diploma or degree could ever make you.

Including mine. All three of them.

Now let's go use them.

Chapter 20: Becoming the Adult That Doesn't Exist

A New Operating System for Life

So here we are. At the end of a book that spent nineteen chapters proving that adults don't exist, the obvious question is: now what?

If no one has it figured out—if the geniuses are guessing, the leaders are improvising, the institutions are failing, the algorithms are exploiting, and the experts are often wrong— does that mean we're all just floating through chaos with no anchor?

No. It means the anchor was never supposed to be another person. It was always supposed to be a process.

. . .

What This Book Gave You

Here's what I want you to take away from these pages. Not a list of rules. Not a motivational speech. Not a five-step framework with a catchy acronym. Just a new way of thinking about what it means to be a person in the world:

Trust processes over personalities. The scientific method, double-blind studies, peer review, independent verification— these are systems designed to work regardless of who's using them. A process that produces reliable results whether it's run by a genius or an intern is infinitely more trustworthy than a charismatic person making gut calls.

Seek disconfirmation, not confirmation. Actively look for evidence that you're wrong. Not because you probably are (though you might be), but because the act of searching strengthens your thinking either way.

Build a team of honest voices, not yes-people. The most valuable person in your life is the one who tells you what you need to hear, even when it's uncomfortable. Find those people. Protect those relationships. Fire the sycophants. Find your Izzy.

Get comfortable with "I don't know." These three words are a complete sentence and a mark of intellectual maturity. Practice saying them. The more you do, the less scary they become.

Evaluate ideas on merit, not source. Listen to uncomfortable truths from people you don't like. Question comfortable lies from people you admire. That's real thinking.

Give yourself permission to be a work in progress. You were never supposed to arrive at some final form of yourself. You were supposed to keep evolving, learning, screwing up, and adjusting.

* * *

The Paradox of This Book

I want to acknowledge the irony of what I've just done. I've written a book telling you not to trust people who write books. I've positioned myself as someone with insight into the human condition while spending twenty chapters explaining that no one can be fully trusted to have insight into the human condition.

Yep. That's the paradox. And I'm okay with it.

Because the point was never "trust me instead." The point was "don't trust anyone instead." Including me. Especially me. Take what's useful from these pages, throw out what isn't, and make up your own mind. That was always the goal. If you finish this book and your primary takeaway is "Ken Konet is really smart," then I've failed. If you finish this book and your primary takeaway is "I need to think more carefully about who I trust and why," then we're good.

The Last Word (For Now)

Adults don't exist. Not in the way we were taught to believe. Not as some final, finished, fully competent version of a human being who has mastered the art of living.

What exists instead is something far more interesting: a species of confused, curious, terrified, hopeful, occasionally brilliant, frequently ridiculous primates who are trying their best with faulty hardware and incomplete information.

Some of us just have nicer chairs.

And that's okay. More than okay. It's wonderful. Because if nobody has it figured out, then you're not behind. You're not broken. You're not failing at some game that everyone else has mastered.

You're human. That's the whole job.

I started this book with a story about my father and a kitchen sink. A man with a wrench and the absolute confidence that turning forty had installed some kind of Home Repair Module in his brain. Twenty minutes later: a geyser. My mother on the phone with a plumber. And a seven-year-old kid learning the most important lesson of his life: the adults are winging it. I'm still that kid. I'm just taller now, with more degrees and better excuses. But the lesson holds. Nobody has the manual. Nobody has the cheat codes. Nobody has the answers, even when they're standing at a podium with a PowerPoint and the unmistakable energy of a person who believes otherwise.

The adults don't exist. But you do. And you're equipped—now more than when you started this book—to navigate the uncertainty without needing someone to pretend they've solved it for you.

Now go be magnificently, imperfectly, beautifully human.

And call a plumber. Seriously. I've seen what happens when you don't.

Acknowledgments

To every person who ever looked at me and thought, "This guy has it together"—I'm sorry for the deception. I was winging it the whole time. Just like everyone else.

To my wife, Izzy, who proves daily that you don't need to have it all figured out to be extraordinary. You just need to show up, roll your sleeves up, and fix things—literally and figuratively. You are the most capable person I know, and you'd be the first to say you're making it up as you go. That's what makes you the best.

To Ibrahim, my co-author on other projects and co-conspirator in the grand experiment of not knowing what we're doing but doing it anyway. Every conversation with you makes me smarter and less certain, which, as this book argues, is exactly how it should work.

To my mother, Paulette, who raised me to question authority while simultaneously being the authority I respected most. That paradox is basically the thesis of this book.

To every genius, leader, icon, and supposed adult whose stories appear in these pages—thank you for being human. Your failures didn't diminish your achievements. They made them real.

And to you, the reader. Thank you for spending time with these ideas. I don't know if this book changed anything for you, and I'm comfortable not knowing. That's kind of the whole point.

About the Author

Ken Konet holds three master's degrees, which sounds very impressive until you remember that this entire book is about how credentials don't automatically make someone an expert at life. He's a corporate instructional designer by day, which means he professionally designs learning experiences for adults—a career built on the deeply ironic foundation of teaching grown-ups how to do things they probably should have figured out already.

Ken is the author of multiple books across genres, all published through Humbolton Press. He lives in Central Florida with his wife Isabella, their collection of projects-in-progress, and the comfortable certainty that neither of them has any idea what they're doing.

He's okay with that. You should be too.

=The End =

www.ingramcontent.com/pod-product-compliance
Lightning Source LLC
Chambersburg PA
CBHW011502260726
48654CB00034B/1937